# BUILD A MASTERMIND!

**I help people start and grow profitable, thriving mastermind communities.**

Join my FREE *BUILD A MASTERMIND CHALLENGE* today!
Click the link below to learn more.

https://buildamastermind.com/challenge

# Praise for Brad Hart and *The 8-Minute Mastermind*

"SINCE THE DAY I met Brad, he's had a strong hand in quite literally reshaping the entire course of my life . . . I don't care if you've been sitting on the fence for six months like I did, or six minutes, it's time for you to step up, invest into your potential, and take a risk that will transform the entire landscape of your life. If you don't, I hope you find some way to escape the traps of unfulfillment, untapped potential, and the gnawing feeling that you're not doing what you want to do."

—ALEX MULLAN

"IT'S BEEN EIGHT weeks with MMM. And I'm not exaggerating when I say my business has been more successful and grown more in the last eight weeks than in the last eight months. The strategic planning, unlimited resources, the network, the personalized mentorship. These are a few ways that MMM has ensured my greatness. But it's the unmatched support from this team and from the other members that has given me the confidence boost I needed to take my business to the next level. They have not only helped me to set the bar high, but they have taken away every barrier and insecurity I might encounter, making success inevitable."

—AMBER TACY

"I attribute THAT to masterminding, and surrounding myself with loving and supportive people, like yourself, and other mentors. This newsletter very much embedded that and today I am extremely grateful for you, your newsletters, the MMM Mastermind, and the RE-recognizing that it is all about the attitude towards the actions, asking the right questions, and always seeking first to understand, and focus on *What is the value that I can add?*"

—STEPHEN VETTER

"ONCE THE MASTERMIND got underway the real magic began to happen. I am being afforded 10 hours a month to work with whatever expert Brad has on his team. I have received so much 1-on-1 time about copy, systems, sales, and lead generation, and that really just scratches the surface of what is available to me. When questioned how much time I have left for consulting, Brad openly says, "take what you need." He truly gives from a place of abundance."

—RYAN CHARABA

"I BET YOU'RE a bit like me, and you've paid for coaches, courses, programs and masterminds that promised the world, but delivered very little "results," leaving you feeling frustrated, helpless, and lost. Or, if you're new to entrepreneurship but don't want to waste years of your life and tons of your hard-earned money on *stuff* that doesn't work, then do your future self a massive favor and reach out to the Make More Marbles team. Brad has surrounded himself with the most capable, qualified, and aligned group of people I have ever encountered."

—JASON GENSLER

"I URGE ANYONE who is looking to create wealth in multiple different streams to align yourself with Brad and the Mastermind. Brad has a wealth of knowledge, experience, and inspiration to help anyone live in theirs dreams. Sometimes, it's the intangibles that propel you the furthest, the fastest. You could never connect the dots looking forward, but when you look back, the little serendipities in life make all the difference."

—JOELY ROBERTSON

"ALL OF THESE blessings have happened for me in LESS THAN 2 MONTHS! The ripple effect of being aligned with Brad and Make More Marbles is that every area of my life is firing on all cylinders. Physical body, emotional mastery, financial mastery, time, my career/mission, and my sense of contribution. All of these area have been accelerated, expanded, and deepened."

—BRAD NEWMAN

"By having access to Brad and his team, a plethora of effective strategies, and the high mindedness of an entrepreneurial community, my revenue has increased, my costs have decreased, and I'm able to maximize some of our current resources, which has added to our bottom line. Ultimately, working with Brad has impacted the most important people in any business—our clients. Our clients are better served because we are able to deliver better and higher quality content on a larger scale so that they can financially transform their lives."

—BRIAN FOUTS

# THE
# 8-MINUTE
# MASTERMIND

BY BRAD HART

BOOKS

*The 8-Minute Mastermind*

*The Choice: Stories of Life, Love, and Learning*

PODCASTS

*The 8-Minute Mastermind Podcast*

*Make More Marbles Podcast*

# THE
# 8-MINUTE
# MASTERMIND

How to Travel Anywhere for Free, Solve any Problem, and Add
$100k+ to Your Business in 5-10 Hours a Month

# BRAD HART

MAKE MORE MARBLES PUBLICATIONS

For information about special discounts for bulk purchases or author interviews, appearances, and speaking engagements please contact:

> Make More Marbles
> 1816 Wading River Manor Road
> Suite 365
> Wading River, NY 11792, United States
>
> Facebook:  fb.me/bradhart
> Messenger: m.me/bradhart
> Email:      support@makemoremarbles.com

First Edition, *Version 3*

Edited, cover design, book design by Rodney Miles: www.rodneymiles.com

# The Mastermind Principle

---

"Now here are some interesting facts about the mastermind which give you an idea of how important it is and how necessary that you embrace this principle and make use of it in attaining success in your chosen occupation.

First of all, it is the principle through which you may borrow and use the education, the experience, the influence, and perhaps the capital of other people in carrying out your own plans in life.

It is the principle through which you can accomplish in one year more than you could accomplish without it in a lifetime if you depended entirely on your own efforts for success."

—NAPOLEON HILL

# Note to Readers

---

This is NOT just a book. It's a multimedia experience—Because sometimes words on paper are just not enough to add all the value (and Make all the Marbles!) that I want to.

For example, to see a great interview where we discuss this book and its title, go here:

http://marbles.link/expertspeaker

So keep an eye as you read for links to additional documents, podcasts, videos, and more which will help you realize the promise of this book in record time! If you need further support to go faster, you can always reach out to:

support@makemoremarbles.com

I love you, thank you for reading.

B

*For Dad*

---

I'VE ALWAYS BEEN interested in solving people's problems. You could call it a savior complex, and you wouldn't be far off. I was always trying to save my dad from himself. He ultimately died alone from complications related to alcoholism. So this is for him, the book I always knew I would one day write, with a technique I've refined over 10,000 hours that truly can help anyone solve any problem.

It is with great pleasure, Dear Reader, that I give it to you. You are a leader, and leaders need tools that solve problems. This is the one tool I would say is worth mastering—whether you use it to travel the world in luxury, build a community of loyal support locally or wherever you find yourself, team up with other leaders to gain exponential results and rewards, or make an additional 6 or 7 figures in your business in 5-10 hours a month.

# CONTENTS

# PREFACE:

# TRANSFORMATION

I WAS BORN in Stony Brook Hospital in August, 1985. The number one song on the billboard charts that year was "Like A Virgin" by none other than Madonna. My head was about as large as it is now when I was born. It was a long labor, over 30 hours. (Thanks, Mom!) I must have come rolling out like a bowling ball with legs. Things went pretty well for a couple years after that. My mom and dad were married, we lived in a small town in eastern Long Island near a lake with a name no one could pronounce except the locals. Mom worked at delis and dad drove a lumber truck. He had been on the job over a decade. One day when I was two years old, a load shifted when coming down a hill, came through the back of the cab and pinned him to the steering wheel. He slipped a disc in his spine and was unconscious. Dad couldn't walk for nearly a year. He had to roll around on a mechanics creeper around the house while he had various surgeries to get him up and walking again. During this time, he made the most fascinating piece of art I've ever seen. I've not seen anything like it before or since. It was a piece of wood with black velvet over it. Small nails were strategically placed all over the board in a pattern. Then, colored stitching thread was used to connect the dots, running through the pins, wrapping around them and making amazing patterns of bright colors. The photo was of a beautiful peacock. My Dad had a lot of issues, but I was close to him toward the end of his life.

He and his brother both had a very artistic lean about them. Uncle Steve created hundreds and hundreds of pieces of original artwork before he died from cancer at the age of 47. Uncle Steve's apartment in New York City was amazing. It was a "classic six"[1] overlooking Broadway on the Upper West Side, lined floor to ceiling with photography and classical music. He used to challenge me to name a composition or ask me what I'd like him to play then abruptly stop the record when I had reached the end of what I could hum of it. He was a playful, giving and caring man. He never showed up empty-handed. His kids (my cousins) and I could never wait to see and eat what he brought. As the GM at Zabar's on the Upper West Side, there was no shortage of amazing food and treats such as smoked salmon, salami, bagels, and other delicacies when Steve was around. I realized many years later that, despite him passing away when I was 8, I felt closest to him out of any members of my family. I mourned his loss in a puddle of tears many years later. I lost grandpa at age 16, and my dad at age

---

[1] Put simply, "classic" refers to prewar architecture and "six" refers to the six rooms. A classic six consists of a living room, formal dining room, kitchen, two bedrooms, and a maid's room (much smaller than the other bedrooms, and usually right off the kitchen). —streeteasy.com

24. All 8 years apart. It makes you see patterns that probably aren't there.

When my dad was injured and could no longer work when I was two, Mom very quickly realized that she couldn't support us working odd jobs at delis and in nursing homes, so she went to the city where everyone in the courts has to start. This meant leaving her five-year-old son behind to make enough money and get the needed medical benefits for us both so we could have a roof over our heads. Dad had disability and social security checks coming, but it was tight. He was an angry alcoholic who never kicked it and it eventually consumed him. She gave me the option at a very young age to stay with him or go. Even at that young age I somehow knew that if I left, he would die (he eventually did anyway, 20 years later). To his credit, he managed to stay off the booze until I was 16.

Growing up there were never many women around. In the neighborhood I grew up in on Long Island, the fairer sex was more rare than fair. My mom was the breadwinner in our family, working as a court officer, which forced her to wear a masculine mask most of the time. They had nicknamed her "the launcher" after she did just that to a guy who wouldn't leave her friend alone at a bar. She was tough as nails and had to make some really hard choices so I, her only son, unplanned but still loved, could survive and thrive. She had worked since she was 13 to support her six younger brothers and sisters.

All the women that were around were very much in their masculine. My grandmother was an incredibly smart woman and an enigma for her time. Way more talented than the norms and mores of the age would allow for. She graduated from William and Mary with a degree in 1933, one of the first women ever to do so, but when she returned to the town in which she was born, the options were to become a schoolteacher or a nurse. She became a schoolteacher, drove herself every day, and smoked. When 30 years was up, she collected her pension, stopped smoking, and stopped driving all on the same day.

Months went by before anyone noticed the change: "Grandma, did you quit teaching? Wait, did you quit smoking? Why don't you drive anymore?" She just never really spent much time complaining.

After my dad and I had our fistfight at age 16 (he blindsided me one morning on a binge after we got into an argument earlier that day) I wouldn't talk to him for months. He spent time in jail and I left, first living in my car then reluctantly moving in with my mom and stepfather, who I was still very much angry at for leaving and not being much a part of my life.

I was an angry kid. Still am sometimes.

And there were really no women around. So I do what most over-masculinized, bullied children of alcoholics might do, I escaped into whatever I could. I got great at guitar very quickly. I masturbated frequently. I drank and smoked pot. I would listen to music or go on the swings to avoid the constant nonsense from the other kids. I just wanted to escape. I dreamed of a life where I could actually talk to girls. Where I could travel outside my little bubble. One day I wished that I would have friends wherever I went. I would treat people right and do everything I could to help them. I would travel the world helping people and being of service.

One day.... The universe heard me and gave me the tools to do exactly that. It started with the first personal development book I ever read: *The Game* by Neil Strauss. It's funny because you wouldn't normally put that book in that category, but it really is. You see, where I was, I was this kid, about 19 at this stage, who had never once had sex. I was a complete disaster around women, I couldn't really even talk to a girl I was remotely attracted to. It took all my courage just to ask a girl out to prom, and thankfully she said yes! I would have been devastated otherwise. So reading that book, and hearing about this entire world I had never even thought could be possible where you can not only talk to women, but date them, have sex with them, marry them, have kids with them, and have them be a part of your life in a meaningful way? That was a dream come true.

And at that time honestly, none of the other stuff that I could have had access to, read, or watched would have done anything to catch my attention. Neil was speaking directly to my pain, in his world-class, artful storytelling way. And as the confidence I gleaned from his work started to turn into evidence of success, I was hooked. I went on to have more wonderful relationships with women than I care to recount. Highs, lows, and everything else. But I was hooked on growth.

Years later, I would join my first mastermind led by Neil, The Society. It was the dream—learn from the man himself and 50 other men about what it means to be a man in today's world. How to become a mix of Jason Bourne, Don Juan, and Brad Pitt. It was incredible. I suddenly had a peer group that I could learn from, some younger, but most way older, who had been through a thing or two. And what was funny was I never actually became a "pickup artist" nor really had any lasting desire to be. Sure I would fantasize about being the guy who could get any girl, but I also had seen the other side of that type of behavior and quickly realized it wasn't all it was cracked up to be. It was just another addiction that led to pain, divorce, heartbreak and a lot of wasted time.

I knew in my soul, even then, that there must be more for me to give, to contribute and to become. And once you have transformed, and mastered the tools of transformation, you can now transform others.

The *mastermind* is the highest impact vehicle to do so.

# DISCOVER THE PODCAST!

Want to hear ME run MY mastermind and get a ton of value from the hot seats while you're at it? Check out the *8-Minute Mastermind Podcast* (Don't forget to rate, subscribe, and share if you like it!).

https://makemoremarbles.com/podcasts/

# INTRODUCTION

"If you have an apple and I have an apple and we exchange these apples then you and I will still each have one apple. But if you have an idea and I have an idea and we exchange these ideas then each of us will have two ideas."

—George Bernard Shaw

# ALEX MULLAN

WHEN I MET Brad, I was living in a town that was slowly killing me inside. I was at a crossroads with what I wanted to do with my life moving forward and was spending 40hrs/week slinging lattes at Starbucks for pennies in comparison to what I knew I was worth. Since the day I met Brad, he's had a strong hand in quite literally reshaping the entire course of my life, and I truly do not believe I'd be where I am today had I not *finally* watched the Wealth Machine videos he did with John Romaniello (after leaving them to fester in my inbox for six months). I find it amusing, and serendipitous that off the back of that video series (which for the record, little applied to me because I live in the Great Land of Canada), Brad and Roman have been the largest influencers in my life and greatest mentors, ever. It's an honor-and-a-half to be able to call you both friends.

Brad, as I sit here writing, staring out at what's the first of what will surely be many West Coast rains over the coming months, for the first time in my life, I'm *excited* to be around these parts for the winter months. I showed you my glorious

Stripe stats, comparing the first 16 days of September to August. I told you that I'm soon to be paying in *rent* what I used to *earn* in an entire month at Uncle Bux. I still can't believe it. If you'd told me on the first fateful phone call we had, that within 2.5 years I'd have gone from being a supervisor at Starbucks, effectively "stuck" in my little hometown, to being able to travel freely, having built what I most accurately describe as a consulting business (given the different tracks I run in) that's on track to hit the 6k mark this month (with 80-85% of that being MRR), I'd have laughed. It seems like a dream, especially since May, June, July, and August were a struggle, with next-to-no movement forward in my business. Once I can figure out how to more effectively streamline the different things I do, eliminate and outsource to free up time, this rocket ship you pointed in the right direction is going to *launch*. Anyway, all this to say, I'm looking at this move to Vancouver as new beginnings (as I'm starting entirely from scratch over there), as well as bringing the push I need to jump up to the next echelon in my life. To quote Kramer, It's all, "Levels, Jerry. Levels."

Personal things and stuff aside, I'm EXCITED about the direction we charted on the phone yesterday. As I said many times, you've had a huge impact on my life, and I know that together we can bring that impact to a whole lotta people and shift the world. When you said that you view me as a partner as opposed to worker, *that meant a lot to me.* Truly, I know you don't say things like that off-hand, and hearing that was deeply appreciated. Serendipitously, I believe it was roughly a year ago when I sent you a similar rambling email about joining you on your Make More Marbles mission. I've gotta say, it's damn cool to see what we've achieved in 365 days. Better yet, on a personal level, the ripple effect to other people in my life has been impactful, and incredible. The increase in my baseline happiness is entirely due to the fact that I'm able to spend much of my time working on projects that excite me. Simply put, I would never have realized this potential and opportunity had Brad not shown me the path.

I don't care if you've been sitting on the fence for 6 months like I did, or 6 minutes. It's time for you to step up, invest into your potential, and take a risk that will transform the entire landscape of your life. If you don't, I hope you find some way to escape the traps of unfulfillment, untapped potential, and the gnawing feeling that you're not doing what you want to do.

—ALEX MULLAN

# THE
# INDISPENSIBLE
# TOOL

IS YOUR CURRENT LIFE the one you envisioned? Is your business where you want it to be? Are you able to travel, to serve at the highest level, to use the talents you are given to impact the world in the way you know you can? Do you have the freedom, the support, the resources, and the game plan that you want to have in place?

No?

Are you a coach, consultant, leader, speaker, author, executive, or entrepreneur? Are you making at least six figures but want to get off the income rollercoaster and start really scaling not only your income but your impact? Maybe you're a leader who's constantly bombarded with requests for mentorship and coaching, but you have neither the time nor the inclination to do it for free? Maybe you just want to have a hell of a lot more FUN in your business than you are experiencing right now?

Yes?

I've made a lot of money in the past *without* helping people and having a lot of fun, and it didn't feel great. In fact, if you study Human Needs Psychology, the only way to have all your needs met is a high-level focus on growth and contribution. Even now, as I'm typing and the words are flowing through me to serve you at the highest level, I know I am guided. I want you to experience this feeling as well—not thinking, not guessing, but knowing that you are guided, that you matter, and that you can make a difference. Life will kick you, hard, and you always have a choice about how to respond. And each time, as you reach another level, you will have to face another devil. That's just how life is.

It never gets easier; you just get better.

*Masterminds* will help you solve any problem whatsoever, enable you to travel anywhere, and to get off the feast-and-famine wheel, creating predictable recurring revenue in your business. They allow you and your clients to create the clarity, accountability, support, and trust you need to achieve any vision you can dream up. Masterminds will allow you to finally visit all the places you've always wanted to go and do it in style—while getting paid!

Most importantly, once you learn this simple step-by-step system, you can go deep with more people, help them transform in ways you won't believe, and find something deep inside yourself that most businesses just can't provide. This model can be run in 10 hours or fewer a month, from anywhere, in person or virtually.

Sounds amazing, right? It is!

But what *is* a mastermind? Mastermind *groups* offer *unmatched and invaluable* opportunities, including:

- Accountability from your peers
- Real-life education
- Brainstorming
- Peer support
- Sharpening your existing skills
- Challenging you to set exciting goals—goals you might not achieve otherwise
- Networking and making new friends
- Travel and new experiences
- Contribution and fulfilment
- In short, *success!*

Masterminds are created and run by *facilitators*, and I'm about to teach you how to be a happy, energized, and financially successful one. Masterminds can be created around a particular subject or a particular goal. Both successes and problems encountered can then be addressed and solved by the group. A diversity of perspectives, ideas, and approaches combined with good team building can be unstoppable and can carve off *years* of trial and error on one's own.

Masterminds require a degree of organization and maintenance, but it's easier than you might think. Following a successful format, masterminds are easy. One big epiphany my students seem to share off the bat is the realization that masterminds are not just something an expert puts together and charges for, but an incredible way for you to *learn something you'd like to master quickly.* I've done this many times and I'll share some of my experiences with you in this book and in my other materials and services. We might even be in a mastermind together, someday.

Masterminds are *not* a classroom, *not* just a networking group—although you might share tips and leads and even form joint ventures (JV)—and they are *not* group coaching. In fact many ask me, "Brad, this is just a fancy group coaching program, right?"

"Nope."

"Well, what's the difference between running a mastermind and just coaching a group?"

Well, first, unlike group coaching, *the people who you serve rely on you for your leadership, as their servant leader.* It's an important distinction to make because although coaching is an incredible way to learn and make an impact, masterminding is decidedly NOT coaching. An average coach is trained to help you gain clarity and push you toward the results you want. But many coaches are not trained at all and get inconsistent results when dealing with clients as a result.

To be an effective coach, I believe you don't need to be the utmost expert, but you do need to be committed to solving people's problems. You can use a mastermind to learn, and you don't need to know everything if you are committed to service and finding the right answers. The best coaches are not only trained to pull the best out of people and get them to make progress based on their own vision, but "walk the walk"—they invest in themselves and are consistently attending to their growth with personal and professional development programs, books, podcasts, events, and training programs.

If I had a dollar for every time I met a "coach" who had zero qualifications to do that job, I would be a much richer man indeed. And the biggest problem with the coaching industry in general is there are so few barriers to entry that anyone who decides they don't like their job can hang out their shingle as a coach and get to work stalling at best and destroying people's lives at worst with their ignorance. Their clients not only don't get the results they were sold on, but they become disillusioned with the entire coaching industry as a result and begin to mistrust everything they need most to transform. Same goes with consultants, they're a dime a dozen today, but the truly great ones are few and far between.

But let's assume that if you're reading this, that's not you. You are a great coach, consultant, leader, speaker, facilitator, or any of the above, and you are the person who *should be* considering starting and leading a mastermind. I assume you have some chops, and I'm here to help you make more impact and income in less time.

*Masterminding is a powerful and thoroughly enjoyable tool for anyone interested in a new model for creating a business you love while freeing your time in the process. Masterminds provide a perfect forum to obtain or leverage knowledge while creating an ever-growing network for greater impact. In addition to a powerful and fast method of becoming an expert in any area you choose, it's a business model with no physical product, no inventory, and which requires very little support to operate. It's a simple method for creating a business where your clients run the delivery and fulfillment, freeing you from having to deliver results each week.*

Several years ago, when I first got started building masterminds, I didn't really know what I was doing or what to expect. And there was a severe lack of resources and tools to help prepare and guide me. So I had to figure it out on my own. I knew masterminds could be a big part of my businesses, but I wasn't sure how to leverage them ... yet. All I knew was that I had a lot of valuable business experience and information and that masterminds could be a good way to share my expertise and increase my income while helping others massively in the process.

So what did I do?

I worked hard to find clients as quickly as possible. Most of my efforts were a huge waste of my time and energy. I was frustrated, exhausted, and had very little to show for my efforts. I tried everything to no avail. So I kept trying new things. I experimented with new ideas, different strategies, and a variety of methods. And I documented everything—the good and the bad. While I wasn't happy with my results early on, I was LEARNING.

And eventually, things started to fall into place. I started to get my first few clients, increase my bank account balance on a predictable basis, and find my groove. Along the way, if something wasn't working, I'd adjust accordingly and fix it. To learn even more, I joined several other masterminds (28 now to date) and took notes on what was and wasn't working. Then I used those experiences to enhance my own mastermind groups. As I kept making tweaks, my masterminds kept growing—slowly at first. But these snowflakes eventually snowballed and turned into avalanches. I noticed that my mastermind members were engaging more with me and with the group. I was connecting with them on a deeper level, and my message started to resonate with them.

And then my mastermind members started seeing MASSIVE results.

It was thrilling! Before I knew it, my income was skyrocketing and my mastermind groups were thriving. Not only had I built a successful mastermind that was generating a significant income, but I was helping other entrepreneurs do the exact same thing! Since then, I've helped thousands of entrepreneurs harness the power of mastermind groups to increase their income and their impact. As I said, I've started many mastermind groups of my own and I have joined countless others as a participant, guest, speaker, and facilitator. I've easily got 10,000 hours of masterminding under my belt now and have honed my process to a razor's edge.

So after extensive research and experience, I know what it takes to create and sustain a thriving mastermind group. It's now my goal to help people just like you build mastermind groups to increase their income and impact exponentially. *And it's way easier than you would think.* Whether you're a coach, leader, speaker, author, executive, or entrepreneur, I can teach you the steps to build your own successful mastermind.

Since 2011 I've joined 28 mastermind groups and started 10 successful ones. During the process, I realized there was a severe lack of training, tools, and resources on how to build a successful mastermind, let alone generate an income from one. That's why I've compiled everything I've learned into a simple process and written this book. I've done the work for you so you don't have to make the same mistakes I did. I wish I had this book when I was first starting out or when I was facing obstacles with my masterminds. It would've saved me a lot of time, money, and trouble. Anyone can implement these steps, and you will experience significant results if you do—just like I did and continue to do.

And I'm going to share my process with you in this book.

Masterminds have been my number one learning tool. I've learned so much, gained so many insights, formed so many powerful partnerships and launched so many incredible projects and initiatives through mastermind groups.

Here's a short list:

- Traveled to over 25 countries and 43 states, much of it paid for by putting on masterminds.
- Launched an Amazon services business and helped bring it from $0 to $75,000 recurring monthly revenue in one year.
- Earned $35,000 for our expert joint venture and gained a priceless free education in sourcing products from China and Hong Kong, along with all my travel paid.

- Started a hedge fund that returned 106% in one year—4x the S&P 500 for that year.
- Joined the board of two charities which together have lifted dozens of communities out of poverty, built homes for the homeless, schools for kids, and fresh water for those in crisis situations.
- Routinely helped others add 6 and 7 figures to their personal income and business revenues.
- Learned business—what works and what doesn't—from the ground up.
- Built a community and network of support that far surpasses anything I could pay to join.
- Have created the 'genie' effect with my network, anything I could ever wish for is just a Facebook post away.

None of this is meant to brag or impress, but to *impress UPON you* what is possible with the power of masterminds. It's to show you that the wish I made at eight years old that day on the swing set *came true,* in large part due to masterminds: I really do have friends now wherever I go in the world. And even when things are challenging, which they sometimes are, I know beyond the shadow of a doubt that the answer is only a text or phone call away *thanks to masterminds.* Even in the midst of health issues and hardship, I am grateful.

I've taken everything I've learned over the years of attending and building successful masterminds and simplified it in this book for you. I want to give you an opportunity to plug and play this model into what you are already doing, so you can bring to bear the unbelievable power of masterminds in all areas of your life. I've got the entire process dialed, from marketing to sales, to delivery, to referrals, to running the meetings, to booking the trips—everything ready to go and plug right in to what you already have going on.

One of my goals is to empower entrepreneurial leaders to build communities of world changers who work together to solve the grand challenges of our times, to light the FUSE— Food, Energy, Shelter, and Education for the most number of people possible. Lofty, right? But when you really see the power of masterminds, you might see how this is actually possible, if not inevitable.

The goal of this book is to get people interested in the concept of masterminding as a way to travel anywhere, solve any problem, and grow your business and network exponentially. I know—I've done it and I'm still doing it every day. You can get some practice under your belt with a free mastermind and move on to paid ones, and right way, like in the next chapter, we're getting started.

So this is the most important tool that I can give to you, a manual on not just why, but *how*. In this book, these are my goals:

1. To teach you everything you need to know to start, run, grow, and improve your own mastermind groups;
2. To enable you to help a lot of people, have a lot of fun, and make a lot of money.

In this book, I will show you...

- How to build and run a mastermind efficiently and effectively.
- How coaches, consultants, leaders, speakers, authors, executives, and entrepreneurs leverage their knowledge and network for greater income.
- A business model with no product, no inventory, and very low capital to start.

- A simple method for generating a primary (or additional) stream of highly profitable revenue in only 5-10 hours per month.
- Where to find clients who will gladly pay you $1,000-$5,000 on a monthly basis. ANSWER? Well, one answer, anyway, is *from your free masterminds*. In fact, you don't have to wait. Study this book, of course, and join my FREE challenge here:

www.buildamastermind.com/challenge

And much, much more . . .

If you have transformed in some way, you might have a keen desire to impact and help others to do so as well, and there are many ways to impact people:

- Videos
- Books
- Social Media
- Events
- Speaking
- Coaching
- Group Coaching
- Online Courses
- Online Communities

But very few of these in my experience provide the scalability and ease of impact and transformation of a mastermind group. Masterminds have a lot of the best qualities of those in the list above without as many of the downsides. They don't, for example, go a mile wide but just an inch deep, and they don't require all of your time to administrate.

I want to give you the one tool in my toolkit that's made the difference for me, time and time again. The one tool that's allowed me to live an amazing life, where I feel grateful every day, even for the pain. And when you can be grateful even for your pain, what the hell can stop you?

So, how do you get started with masterminds?

That's easy.

Start a *free* one, first.

# BUILD A MASTERMIND!

**I help people start and grow profitable, thriving mastermind communities.**

Join my FREE *BUILD A MASTERMIND CHALLENGE* today!
Click the link below to learn more.

# I. INVENT YOUR

# MASTERMIND

"If you want to go fast, go alone. If you want to go far, go together."

—AFRICAN TRIBAL SAYING

# RYAN CHARABA

WHEN I MET Brad I was about a year out of the military. I was in the process of getting my business started and I was utterly by myself. My business was a legal entity and I had a couple of clients, yet I was stabbing in the dark at the other 75% of my business that I had no idea about. Once I got set up with Brad he began to teach me at a basic level the things he believed were key to successful business building. There was no assumption about my abilities and we built a relationship from the ground up. And even though he was the teacher I always felt like an equal.

Once the mastermind got underway the real magic began to happen. I am being afforded 10 hours a month to work with whatever expert Brad has on his team. I have received so much 1-on-1 time about copy, systems, sales, and lead generation, and that really just scratches the surface of what is available to me. When questioned how much time I have left for consulting, Brad openly says, "take what you need." He truly gives from a place of abundance.

I have been able to double the asking price for my services. I am able to give way more of myself to my clients because all of my systems and back end are expertly supported by Brad and his team. This has truly increased my reach and my ability to truly help more people than I ever really thought possible. If I had not signed on with Brad I would still be stabbing around in the dark of solo-preneurship. Since meeting I am on the cusp of publishing my first book, booked speaking gigs, and I have doubled my income. Working with Brad and his team is proving every day that I haven't even scratched the surface.

It is quite possible that this is the one thing that could propel you and your potential to the next level. Do not hesitate to invest in yourself. You will not regret it.

—RYAN CHARABA

# WHO, WHAT, AND WHAT IF?

## WHO ARE YOU?

We've all heard that question before. Won't be the last time, either. But we are not the same. People have a lot of things in common. It helps so that we can relate to each other. Everything happens for a reason. You may not believe this now but you will.

*You must discover who you actually are before we can begin.*

It doesn't take living with monks in China or at an Ashram in India, although that certainly couldn't hurt. It doesn't matter where you go, because there YOU are. If you're struggling here, you'll be struggling there. Trust me, I know from experience. If YOU don't learn who YOU are, you can never do what YOU were meant to do here in this crazy place we all find ourselves in. We each have a piece of the puzzle of this beautiful mosaic that we call life. It's yours. No one else can do it like you can. They can come close, but in a universe with variables as infinite as the possibilities of the arrangement of atoms, you are extremely unique. You are the only you. Forever. You will never be again. And you have an expiration date.

So who are you? Are you an artist? A creative? A systems person? Do you love building teams? Do you love to enroll people in your schemes, visions, and plans? Do you only feel alive when you're taking risks? Can you sell anything to anybody at any time?

Great!

You got it. Hold on to that vision of yourself for a moment and take note of which of the things I just described resonated with you most. We're going to need that in a second.

## Next, **WHAT DO YOU WANT?**

What if you had no limits, if you were unstoppable, if you were smarter than the collective whole of humanity?

Yes, *you*.

I don't care if you flunked biology. I want to know what that spark is. I want to tease it out of you. I want to know what YOU think the future *should* look like. Is it an abundant future? Do people prosper and live in harmony? Is it a dystopia? Are people suffering and living in fear—even more than they already are now? Are kids growing up safe? Are hurt people still hurting *other* people? Or did you stop the cycle? Did you take action? Did you figure out what you wanted to contribute to the world and act on it?

Well, I might have bad news—

## THE INDIVIDUAL HAS NO POWER

Only when we join forces can we effect change on a massive scale. Never has anyone achieved anything of note without the participation or at least the passive consent of others somewhere along the way. Stop being a tragic hero. The world needs your gifts too badly to play small or stay isolated. The world needs you to win. If we all stepped up and joined forces we would have a "neotopia" tomorrow.

## BELIEFS

If I handed you a hot coal, what would you do? Drop it? Are you sure? What if you were cold? What if that coal kept you safe and warm for a long time? Maybe that coal used to be a part of the fire that served you and your family and your tribe and community for the longest time, but now that it's being held tightly in your palm, it's burning you and you can't let it go? Such are our beliefs. Here's an example:

Belief: "What can I do? I'm just one person."

FALSE! You are everyone. We are all one.

You are a key and integral part of the puzzle. You are the one who can pick up the ball and run it into the end zone, but not without blockers, tacklers, linebackers, linemen, wide receivers. You get the idea. You just need to find your team and protect your own. Create emotional juice, energy, whatever you want to call it, for and with your TEAM. That's the stuff that will lead your team to victory. Practice creating it daily—first in yourself and then in others. Make it a habit. Work the muscle until it hurts and force it to grow. You'll need every ounce of it for the journey ahead. Because there be dragons on this path were walking.

Beliefs that we hold on to irrationally that ultimately do not serve us do more harm than a fire ever could. They keep us playing small and not sharing our gifts out of fear or uncertainty. They are exactly the things we need to identify and drop so we can stop the damage they are causing.

You deserve to share your gifts. The world needs and deserves them. To not share your gifts would be selfish and pointless. That doesn't serve anyone.

So let go of that coal. Now.

What is it for you?

- "I don't know where to begin."
- "I'm too young or old."
- "I don't know the right people."
- "I don't have the resources."
- "I'm already happy."
- "I don't care about money."
- "I'm an artist/creative/hippy/walrus/gumshoe, koo-koo-ka -choo?"

## WHAT IF YOU COULDN'T FAIL?

Because I'm suggesting *you can't,* not with a great mastermind behind you. And that's the mindset I'd like you to have going in to this.

First, decide the purpose of your mastermind. Is there some area you'd like to learn about or master? You can jump-start your mastering it with a mastermind. Or, is there an area you *are already* expert in and you'd like to share that expertise (for income or for free), develop it further, or position yourself publicly as an expert in that field?

The point is once you understand the value and potential and capabilities of a mastermind, even before you know the mechanics of running one, you can and should decide on what the purpose of the mastermind (MM) will be—more sales for your business or practice? Conquering some major life or business issue? Becoming an expert? Leveraging your expertise for added income?

Look around and see what other masterminds are doing and THINK BIG in inventing your own. Once you have a bright idea, GET EXCITED, and START!

# 2. CREATE YOUR GROUP

"The Master Mind Principle: Two or more people actively engaged in the pursuit of a definite purpose with a positive mental attitude, constitute an unbeatable force."

—NAPOLEON HILL

# JASON GENSLER

I FIRST REACHED out to Brad Hart in early 2017 through Facebook messenger. I was really struggling to find people who could catalyze our social ventures (nonprofits) to a level that I had been envisioning for years but not producing. Brad set up a Zoom call with me for free without hesitation. What I appreciated most about Brad was that he didn't waste any time telling me exactly what I needed to hear. He made sure I understood specifically why he was suggesting I do things a certain way in the future and why what I was currently doing wasn't working. Then he basically said, "Now go do this and don't even think about reaching back out to me until you have done what I suggested, because you just admitted that it's possible and you are confident that you can accomplish it."

Six months later, we had the pleasure of receiving a message from Frank Eric Cimrhanzel and he offered to do a Breakthrough Strategy Session with us for free because we had some amazing opportunities being presented to us. So of course, we agreed. After our call with Frank, our whole team looked at each other, totally blown away. We realized that we got more out of that one 30-minute call with Frank that was FREE than we'd gotten from over $30k in "coaching" and "programs" and "masterminds" during the previous year!

Three months later I asked Brad to join the advisory board for our nonprofits. We celebrated when after many weeks of Brad conducting his due diligence to be sure it was a good fit, not just for us, but for him as well, he agreed. Point is, we have accomplished more in the last nine months as an organization, than what had been accomplished in the previous four years. I recently had a quick 10-minute call on a Sunday morning with Brad, because I needed his advice. Not even a week later, we were launching yet another program in our business and the projections for the proceeds we will generate and the amount of people we will help is outrageous.

I bet you're a bit like me, and you've paid for coaches, courses, programs and masterminds that promised the world, but delivered very little "results," leaving you feeling frustrated, helpless, and lost. Or, if you're new to entrepreneurship but don't want to waste years of your life and tons of your hard-earned money on "stuff" that doesn't work, then do your future self a massive favor and reach out to the Make More Marbles team. Brad has surrounded himself with the most capable, qualified, and aligned group of people I have ever encountered.

Brad and his team will absolutely blow your mind with how efficiently they guide you to achieving your wildest dreams in record time. Thank You Brad and everyone at Make More Marbles for all that y'all do for others.

—JASON GENSLER

# FIND AND GROW
# YOUR TRIBE

WE WILL BE focusing on building a FREE mastermind in your local community, using a Facebook group as a hub. I started mine in 2018 and it has quickly ballooned to almost 425 members, and we routinely have 20-25 attendees each week. I've also been a part of 28 masterminds now (free to $100k/year) and started eight of my own (free to $25k/year) so I can help you with monetizing masterminds with my Build a Mastermind (BAM) Program. It's like a mastermind for masterminds. Visit

www.buildamastermind.com/challenge to get started.

We've rented a really beautiful space and we're adding a monthly entrepreneurial mixer. And if you ever find yourself in San Diego on a Wednesday, reach out!

support@makemoremarbles.com

I've always said that masterminds are the number one tool in my entrepreneurial toolkit. Everything I have accomplished has been a function of the teams I've built, mostly due to the mastermind networks of which I've been a part:

- Our Amazon company quickly went from an idea last year to $400k in recurring revenue.
- Our hedge fund not only had a $1,040,000 month, but returned 106% inside one year, quadrupling the S&P.
- I've helped companies double their revenue and install a giving program inside of three months so they can be in alignment with the laws of affluence and abundance and finally thrive.
- All the hundreds of impact projects, trips to exotic destinations, thousands of relationships, and more.

If I had to throw out every other method of becoming successful, I would keep masterminds. I've even started my own now in my home that meets weekly, to serve the entrepreneurs of the community at no cost (save snacks).

By the way, the one thing that remains elusive to most people who join masterminds—which I'll mention right here in the beginning—is something that took me a long time to learn. They go to the masterminds, they meet all these wonderful people, but their follow up game is weak sauce. They don't understand, just because you have tactics, just because you have access, DOES NOT mean you have the key pieces to be in the big time. You might be missing one key and critical skillset that differentiates the mediocre from the world-class, and that's the art and science of *deal making*.

Making the right deal is the key to success or failure in life, because rarely is anything of merit accomplished alone. You can't start something without access to the resources, skills, and expertise that you need. *Masterminds* provide so much of that, but *people* are the key to all wealth. Their access, when coupled with yours, mitigates risk, and multiplies success exponentially. So you need people who know, like, trust you, and are aligned with your values, incentivized, and have skin in the game alongside you. You also want to make sure these people have exactly what they need to be successful, and redundancy behind them so they can continue to expand, get leverage and produce more.

It truly is an art, the art of people, understanding how they think, what they want (hint, it's not just money) and a true love of service and giving. You must build the bridges that will stand the test of time. I've mastered this skill over many years and decades of practice and the results speak for themselves. I know dozens of levers I can pull to start, grow, and sell a business, taking on very little personal risk. But I too still have a lot to learn.

A great mastermind participant—and definitely a great mastermind facilitator—will end up with a network which is vast, relationships which are deep, and the experience to add 6-7 figures to your business in record time through warm connections. That's all INSANELY valuable in business and in life. It's staggering—the value that can be provided by knowing the right people at the right time. What would it be like to have the best connectors in the world working on your behalf every day to help you crush your goals?

"That would be amazing," you say. "Think of how much I could get done if I had this dynamic duo on my team."

And you'd be correct.

What can one person do? Well not much. That's why building a tribe is so important. How do you build a tribe? Same as we always have, it just seems as though some people have forgotten. Or maybe their outside influences have downplayed its importance. It's the oldest trick in the book: Divide and conquer.

Here's a refresher on how to build a tribe:

- Identify and build your strengths (don't worry, it's easier than you think).
- Add as much value as possible.
- Give first and give abundantly.
- Crush your scarce and limiting beliefs.
- Act as everyone you meet is part of your tribe, whether they agree or not is irrelevant.
- Help everyone get where they need to go next.
- Ask others to pay it forward.
- Ask for help when you need it.
- Stop competing, start evolving.
- Make better trades, bets, decisions and choices.
- Determine what you are willing to lose and stick to it (stop-loss).
- Cut your losers once the stop loss is reached.
- Learn to love failure and never fail to learn.
- Constantly seek to refine your paradigms in the light of new information.
- Embrace who you actually are, loving yourself unconditionally.
- Build assets, limit liabilities.
- Define what you need and limit wants.
- Don't bother trying to grab at the marbles. Make more marbles.
- Aim bigger, achieve more.

Surrounding yourself with a tribe of people who are strong where you are weak will allow you and everyone in that tribe to thrive. This is how humans were meant to function, that is the way we evolved. We still evolve today, every day. Less in a

Darwinian sense, but certainly constantly changing based on the results of our choices. We change and refine our paradigms. We create the world we perceive as the result of our trades whether we know or realize or care. Once we wake up to this fact, accepting the risk and responsibility, we can truly be free to design a life we love to live.

At first, this is frightening. But remember always, fear is your ally. You just don't understand yet. It's all up to you and this is scary, but also liberating. But don't fear, we are going to help you build your tribe, so your weak spots won't matter. We are going to help you help yourself so you aren't held back by your current limitations. We are going to help you to be the best version of yourself and learn a framework through which anything becomes truly possible.

Are you excited?

I am!

Let's get started.

## 1.   CREATE A FACEBOOK GROUP

For your first, free mastermind, start by creating a *group* on Facebook. If you need instructions on this, click here:

- https://www.facebook.com/help/1679707199312
  13?helpref=about_content

## 2. ANNOUNCE IT BROADLY

Tweet, share, email, carrier pigeon, smoke signals—whatever will send your announcement of your FREE MASTERMIND furthest fastest and to as many people as possible. Shout this from the proverbial rooftops of internets everywhere. We don't seek to gain monetarily at first because money would just slow it down, we just want this paradigm to be communicated to a larger audience. They can do with it as they wish, including hear it and completely reject it. It's free and it deserves to be. So please share and get ready for the ride of your life. Besides, what's the point of being on top of the mountain and having no one to share it with?

Beyond this first announcement, all of the marketing for my local mastermind group has been 1:1 or referral so far. I used to do coffee dates and meet people for meals, but I learned something about myself: I hate small talk, and I want to go deep and form relationships with people as quickly as possible. Eventually, you just get too busy to do it all 1:1. So I had to switch up my strategy.

As I meet people, I no longer suggest or accept a coffee invitation, I quickly plug them into the mastermind community (my free Facebook group, which is here, by the way: https://www.facebook.com/groups/mastermindsforentrepreneurs/) and invite them to that. This is a key point of leverage in my life that allows me to serve people at a high level, go deep, support the community, and plug people into the already established flow, not having to create it from scratch with each individual. The magic that comes from it is hard to describe. But as long as you continue to share and allow for it to expand it will. People want community more than anything else, as it meets all our needs in a positive way.

When you meet someone that is in your demographic and a good fit for what you're doing, gain their enrollment into the idea of them coming to a mastermind, then ask for their phone number and immediately text them a few things:

1.  Your full name

2.  A link to your FB profile (for example, https://www.facebook.com/bradhart)

3.   A link to your group (for example, here's our local one, if you find yourself in San Diego): https://www.facebook.com/groups/sandiegomastermind)

*A quick note, as a backup to the Facebook group (in case Facebook changes change their algorithm again), make sure you get emails and phone numbers of members as well, so you can still contact them.*

## 3. LET IT GROW

Once your list has grown, it's time to announce and invite them to your first actual mastermind meeting.

# 3. PLAN YOUR

# MEETING

# JOELY ROBERTSON

AS A FRIEND of Brad's for many years, I'd noticed that Brad increasingly became a source of inspiration through his Make More Marbles blog posts and the things he shared on his Facebook wall, stories about connecting people, living life, and basically, being happier. As a natural introvert "accumulator" type, I've always had difficulty opening up to others about my personal and professional challenges. I was inspired and motivated but I felt like I was going at everything alone. My life changed the day I decided join the Make More Marbles Mastermind. Since joining, I've had the opportunity to meet wonderful people from all over the world. The chats I've had with Stijn, Ryan, Brad, and many other members, as well as Brad Newman's awesome story inspires me to think outside the box.

Brad is the kind of guy who just puts his heart out there (pun intended) and loves bringing people together. After joining the MMM Mastermind, I've found a group of friends who are all passionate about living life, getting ahead, and helping each other. The mastermind has opened me up to try different things and it's helped a lot. For example, I had what would seem like a devastating blow where I lost 18 grand in Forex in September! Typically, I would have beaten myself up and been afraid to put any more skin in my investment game. Thankfully, I had my monthly mastermind call a few days later. After chatting with everyone in the mastermind and Brad, I was able to blow it off easily and I'm already back on the horse. He's got a way of helping people put things in perspective.

Brad has inspired me to the point where now I've researched and got in contact with a local group in Australia with a new trading method after my last failure. Whilst that had nothing to do with Brad directly, getting on the masterminds helps me get out of my introvert side and thus reaps rewards.

The calls are so helpful because Brad "gets it." He ran a hedge fund and can share insights and war stories that help me keep my ego in check. That's why I don't mind getting on the calls in the middle of the night, as I live on the other side of the world. In fact, I look forward to them, as I always come away with something valuable. The Mastermind's library of resources is a great place to go for tools and information for getting ahead and living a happy fulfilled life. I look forward to the mastermind call each month, to bounce off new ideas to a fantastic group of people, and to help others with their journey as well. Brad and the Mastermind have given me the courage to access the parts of myself I need in order to keep moving forward in my journey.

I urge anyone who is looking to create wealth in multiple different streams to align yourself with Brad and the Mastermind. Brad has a wealth of knowledge, experience, and inspiration to help anyone live in theirs dreams. Sometimes, it's the intangibles that propel you the furthest, the fastest. You could never connect the dots looking forward, but when you look back, the little serendipities in life make all the difference.

—JOELY ROBERTSON

# MASTERMIND EVENT PLANNING 101

WE WANT A big, happy, successful mastermind, and in ways that means we need to plan for some small but important details as well. These tips are for facilitating a mastermind meetup locally, in-person:

- You'll want to have some snacks for people. In this case, since it's a free mastermind, encourage people to each bring something pot-luck style.
- Get a basic digital timer on Amazon or use the timer on your phone.
- Have plenty of water.
- Have signs telling people to take off their shoes, where the bathroom is, what areas are off limits, and so on.

You don't want to have to interrupt the flow to tell people where things are.

- If people arrive late (it happens) encourage them to grab a seat with a smile and a hand gesture.
- People should sit in a circle facing each other, so that nobody's back is to anyone, in whatever way that makes the most sense given the space.
- And have fun! This should be a joyous part of your week, which you look forward to and so does everyone else.

Find a quiet, large, and private a space as possible. Having it in our home was quickly capping out after a while, so we started hosting it at local restaurants. As long as you buy food, most restaurants are happy to host you. It's far preferable to having it in your home from a clean-up and privacy perspective but does decrease the intimacy. It's annoying to be interrupted by food ordering and runners calling out, but again, there will always be trade-offs. The music is usually the biggest issue, so find a private room and turn it off if possible. Some restaurants are really obtuse about this, playing music loud at all the time. Recently we decided to rent a space I found and we moved to a donation model for the mastermind to recoup the cost. So far, so good.

The intention is a physical space and an atmosphere where people can come together and collaborate, creating more for everyone instead of just competing with one another. This type of group work is life-changing. It's a really powerful framework that I've perfected over many years, being a part of so many masterminds and starting so many myself. Thousands upon thousands of people have transformed their lives and businesses through this model.

Also, when your mastermind gets big, you'll see a lot of hangers-on start to listen in and want to join. This can be negative or positive, depending. If this worries you, see the section on troubleshooting that follows

Once you have an event and a location, you want to make sure you put all the possible details of parking, logistics, what to bring, what to expect, and a brief overview of what you'll be doing, your communication preferences, etc. You don't want to leave anything to interpretation, and you will have to continue to refine this over time. You *will* learn more and more as issues come up and you resolve them.

Now that you have a populated Facebook group to appeal to, here are (Facebook, in this case) a few sample posts for both in your home, at an outside venue, or a virtual mastermind that you can borrow and tweak to suit you.

To download sample posts, see

https://mrbls.co/MMFEEventPost.

Also, by sharing these sample posts you can see an example mastermind agenda and jump right into some of the nomenclature. For example, a "hot seat" is when a group member is asked questions by the facilitator and the facilitator and the group then brainstorm ("mastermind," as a *verb*) with that person. In a large group you have to limit the number of available hot seats, but in a small (often paid) mastermind it's possible for *all* members to have a hot seat (with meetings generally three hours with the last hour allocated for networking).

Hot seats are valuable. When someone enunciates their problem or question, they are naturally gaining clarity, and the collective brainstorming and addressing of the issue(s) raised introduces a ton of creativity, naturally leaving the hot-seat

member with more ideas and solutions than they would have
ever come up with alone.

## Sample Invite (In-Home)

Hey Gang!

***Just a heads up this will be the last mastermind hosted by me until at least December!!*** Details below. I will NOT be responding to calls and texts the day of, so please read the instructions.

PLEASE RSVP (hot seat or not)
First 10 RSVPs are open for hot seats. If you would NOT like a hot seat, totally cool, just add a comment indicating that.

WHAT TO BRING
Please bring a healthy snack or send a few "friends and family" bucks to bradhartholdings@gmail.com via PayPal or @makemoremarbles on Venmo if you can't make it to the store. Please: as much as we love pets, our roommates are allergic so please DO NOT bring them.

If you would care to help me clean up afterward, I would be most grateful. I'm also expanding the time and keeping it looser so people don't stress about traffic. Please bring a notebook, an open mind, and think of something you want to celebrate, a challenge you have, and a question or two you've been pondering.

HERE'S THE FORMAT:
- Brief intro (30 seconds)
- Gratitude/celebrations
- Challenge or current initiative
- Clarifying questions from group
- Connections, resources, opportunities, people, systems, suggestions etc.
- Follow up with that person from the group if we run out of time.

When I say we have to move on, we do. Please be respectful of everyone's time and take a note to follow up with that person afterward. I just text them during or follow up with them after if I don't have their number.

Mi casa es su casa during this time. This is a safe, private space. Treat it with the same sense of privacy and respect that you would your own home. Please consider others and their desire for privacy—do not share anything that happens inside of the room outside of the room without the consent of all concerned and all it may affect.

Listen more than you talk and be considerate of others and where they are at in their journey.

Please if you can't follow these simple rules, I will have to disinvite you. So follow them.

LOGISTICS
<<Fill in address>> is the address. It's a little tricky to find since we live on a side road just off the main road. There's a gap in the addresses on <<street>> and a long driveway-looking road with a large gray apartment-sized mailbox at the end. Park on the street, then walk in there and make a left we're the last house.

PARKING
Please DO NOT park in our driveway. Please park on the street and walk down... you'll see what I mean when you get here. There isn't any room in our driveway for guests, but street parking is plentiful. Our neighbors will complain if you take their parking spots.

Please be a good neighbor and be quiet when entering and exiting the property.

Lastly, enjoy! This is something I have done professionally for many years and normally charge a LOT of money. I do this for no cost as a service to the community on my own time and own dime because it's one of the most powerful tools I have to give. It's meant to foster community, and create clarity, accountability, connections, opportunities and more. But like anything in life, you get out what you put in, so surrender to what is, show up with enthusiasm and positive intent to serve your community and be open to both giving and receiving unconditionally. You'll be surprised and delighted at what happens in this room when you show up fully and take it seriously.

Don't let me forget to take a group photo!

Magic awaits!

See you soon,

B

## Sample Invite (Outside Venue)

Hey Gang!

Please note there is a NEW VENUE this week. Excited to keep this mastermind train rolling! Here's the dizzle my bizzles: We will be meeting at our usual 6-9pm time at <<location>> in<<town>>. I have no idea about parking... do your best! They are offering us a private space free of charge... with one caveat—They are a business, so they want to sell food and drinks.

If you attend, instead of bringing snacks you MUST order something in the $10-15 range. They have a wide variety of options from healthy to sinful. If you are not hungry, you can simply order something delicious for everyone to share. If we are under on our bill, we will not be able to keep coming back.

Please no alcohol consumption during the mastermind. Let's keep our heads and intentions clear. After 8, if you are so called, have at it.

We have space for 15 or so people, possibly more. I haven't seen the room yet so will update.

The best part... NO CLEAN UP! YAY!

I missed you all and I can't wait to see your bright shining faces at the mastermind!

I will NOT be responding to calls and texts the day of, so please read the instructions.

PLEASE RSVP (hot seat or not) so Alisa (who hooked up the sweet deal on the space, woot!) can let them know how many we expect. First 10 RSVP's are open for hot seats. If you would NOT like a hot seat, totally cool, just add a comment indicating that.

WHAT TO EXPECT:
There will be two hours of masterminding and an hour of open networking. Please bring a notebook, an open mind, and think of something you want to celebrate, a challenge you have, and a question or two you've been pondering.

HERE'S THE FORMAT:
- Brief intro if it's your first time (30 seconds)
- Gratitude/celebrations (30 seconds)
- Challenge or current initiative you need support with
- Clarifying questions from group

- Connections, resources, opportunities, people, systems, suggestions etc.
- Follow up with that person from the group if we run out of time.
- Work with each other to create accountability, support, stakes, whatever you need to ensure that you take action toward your goals until you succeed.

## A NOTE ON TIME KEEPING

When I say we have to move on, we do. Please be respectful of everyone's time and take a note to follow up with that person afterward. I just text them during or follow up with them after if I don't have their number.

This is a safe, private group. Treat it with the same sense of privacy and respect that you would your own home with your friends and family. Please consider others and their desire for privacy— do not share anything that happens inside of the room outside of the room without the consent of all concerned and all it may affect.

Listen more than you talk and be considerate of others and where they are at in their journey.

Please if you can't follow these simple rules, I will have to disinvite you. So follow them.

Lastly, enjoy! This is something I have done professionally for many years and normally charge a LOT of money. I do this for no cost as a service to the community on my own time and own dime because it's one of the most powerful tools I have to give.

It's meant to foster community, and create clarity, accountability, connections, opportunities and more. But like anything in life, you get out what you put in, so surrender to what is, show up with enthusiasm and positive intent to serve your community and be open to both giving and receiving unconditionally.

You'll be surprised and delighted at what happens in this room when you show up fully and take it seriously.

Don't let me forget to take a group photo!

Magic awaits!

See you soon,

B

I now send out invites every Monday and they usually book out within an hour or two. Keep at it!

# Build a Mastermind!

**I help people start and grow profitable, thriving mastermind communities.**

Join my FREE *BUILD A MASTERMIND CHALLENGE* today!
Click the link below to learn more.

**👥 BUILD A MASTERMIND**

https://buildamastermind.com/challenge

# 4. START YOUR

# MEETING

# BRAD NEWMAN

I'VE ALWAYS WANTED to be an entrepreneur because I believe it is the best way for me to create my own destiny. Being an entrepreneur allows me to express myself freely through my skills, to give back to my community on a massive level, and to have fun with whomever I'd like. However, for years I was just a "wanna-preneuer" paralyzed by fear, succumbed by drug use, and wasting tens of thousands of dollars on online programs that taught me the "right" system to make money. Before I met Brad, I was making $12 dollars per hour in the addiction services field. I was having a tremendous amount of fun, creating a lot of impact, however I was making an embarrassing amount of money. I've followed Brad on Facebook and read his emails for the last two years, always so intrigued by his authenticity.

I was personally introduced to Brad at his onsite mastermind, the day before Tony Robbin's Unleash the Power Within event in Newark, NJ, in July 2017. I knew *immediately* I was in the right place. Brad was presenting on wealth creation, collaboration, the entrepreneurial wealth cycle, and personal development. These were the topics of life I desired so deeply to understand but I had no understanding of. I knew I needed to know more.

The same day I met Brad Hart, I decided to join his Make More Marbles Mastermind. I was feeling full of excitement and fear—excited to be aligned with someone who can more clearly articulate the problems in my head better than I can, fearful of investing money *again* into an opportunity. There was a tug a war going on inside of me. Is this the best financial decision for me? How am I going to afford this? What is my family going to say?

Blah Blah Blah… If I live in my head, I'm dead. If I live in my heart, all is possible. The heart is the creative force of the universe. In *my* heart of hearts this is what I know: I'm willing to do ANYTHING, invest ANYTHING, be ANYTHING that will increase my quality of life, helps me grow, and allowed me to impact more people. So I signed on the dotted line for his Mastermind. And as people say… the rest is history.

In the 55 days since joining the Make More Marbles Mastermind and being aligned with Brad Hart's mission, these are the physical things that have manifested in my life:

- Celebrating three years clean from all mood-and-mind-altering drugs.
- I have been hired by Scott Oldford, who is a top influencer in the digital marketing/e-learning space.
- The opportunity is virtual so I get to travel the world and work wherever I please, which has always been a dream of mine.
- I have two opportunities to move out west — to either Denver, Colorado or San Diego, California. I've never lived anywhere else besides New Jersey!
- I have tripled my personal income because of multiple opportunities being thrown (literally) my way. I've had to turn some down!

- I am now crystal clear on WHO I AM and how I can contribute. I am supporter, a bridge builder, and a connector. My flow state is PEOPLE, not systems :). Now I build every wealth creation opportunity off of that knowing.

Brad Hart has asked me to join the Make More Marbles team, which is an honor to be aligned with his mission. Now I get to help guide other entrepreneurs/solo-preneurs/intra-preneurs, like myself, to *see*, *be*, and *act*, in the abundance of life. I have a personal mentor who is teaching me the skill of high-ticket sales. He has five years of experience in five different niches and all he wants to do is give me his knowledge freely.

All in 55 days…

Days.

Not decades.

Not years.

Not even all of Q3 2017.

All of these blessings have happened for me in LESS THAN 2 MONTHS! The ripple effect of being aligned with Brad and Make More Marbles is that every area of my life is firing on all cylinders. Physical body, emotional mastery, financial mastery, time, my career/mission, and my sense of contribution. All of these area have been accelerated, expanded, and deepened.

This is the best way to describe Brad Hart: a vortex of energy that connects the highest quality ideas and people for the good of the human race.

I have learned the highest form of honoring myself is to invest in myself; invest in myself with time and invest in myself with money. My willingness to invest in myself has always been there. The difference in investing with Brad is that I'm seeing a return on my investment quicker than I thought imaginable. It's truly remarkable.

The cost of not working with Brad is nothing more than a slower pace in business and in life. A struggle for resources. A constant fear of living in scarcity. A lack of connections. You're the one who has to live with it. Not me :)

If you're already willing to honor yourself, do it by aligning yourself with Brad. If you're ready to accelerate your business and life, do it by aligning yourself with Brad. If you're ready to feel the fulfillment you've been longing for, do it by aligning yourself with Brad.

—BRAD NEWMAN

# START WITH LEADERSHIP IN MIND

LEADERSHIP IS THE most important thing you need to focus on. If you as the leader aren't adding a ton of value, the mastermind will quickly fizzle. We are a business-focused mastermind, so if you are looking to start one that specifically focuses on that, it helps to have experience from which to draw from. That being said, I mastermind on all types of things, from all areas of life—health, wealth, relationships, and more. The format works regardless of the issue. Read it thoroughly and implement it until it's natural.

In that room, I simply want to facilitate from a place of spirit, not ego, and listen to what these incredible men and women have to say. Perhaps add a question from time to time, perhaps posit a problem to discuss, but mainly, just facilitate.

I have seen the process work so many times that it's a foregone conclusion that it will solve any problem with clarity, accountability, support, and trust. And on anything that's stuck leverage and engagement are key—Remember, CASTLE (Clarity, Accountability, Support, Trust, Leverage and Engagement) are the six parts of an effective mastermind, and it's up to you to sharpen your saw to become the leader that can make that happen for everyone.

The key distinction is not to push, not to even pull, but to *lead* the group in a process that works, to facilitate their transformation by getting them in the room and having them stick to the program. Your particular skill set is less relevant, and as long as you stick to the program, you can't fail. It's 99% effective when you just follow the steps and check the boxes. Just like AA, it works if you work it. And as you see people transform before your eyes, crush challenge after challenge, and make incredible progress toward their goals, you'll begin to rely on the process more and more even when people struggle a bit in the interim.

When you can get out of your own way and just trust the process, magic happens.

## LOGISTICS

We started the mastermind in my home, so I made signs to direct people to take off their shoes, join us upstairs, and what bathroom to use and where. You can't be too clear and specific in your expectations. I've had to uninvite people because they park like jerks, make too much noise and the neighbors complain, or bring pets after a clear warning. This is your space, so protect it accordingly. Be the leader.

I've made signs to direct people in my home, which I can easily put up when it's time to rock. I made sure I ate beforehand so I didn't consume only snacks, I'll bring out the trash cans to make sure people can clean up after themselves as they go. I'll make sure the room is comfy, clean and well-lit. We're blessed to have a spectacular view of the ocean, so that definitely helps round out the decor.

When people ask, "Can I bring someone to the mastermind?" I say the only criteria is: "Would you invite this person into your home?" Because if not, they have no business being in mine.

If offsite, remind them to order food so the restaurant doesn't disinvite you in the future. If you end up renting a space specifically for this purpose (which we eventually did) then make sure the ground rules for that space are clear.

Before and at the start I prep people (and myself) for my free, local mastermind. As you've seen, I include logistical information such as address, parking instructions, no pets, bring a healthy snack, and so on. I go through these points quickly at the beginning of each mastermind for about 3-5 minutes to make sure everyone is on the same page, and that saves way more time than addressing these issues later, trust me!

## START THE MEETING

Start out the meeting with the following:

- Welcome everyone.
- Remind them of logistics, bathroom, water, trash, etc.
- I then often say something like, "I'll be sharing some of my ground rules to make this a successful evening, and hopefully continue to have these as an ongoing service to the community. First and foremost: This is NOT the Brad Hart show! I am hosting and facilitating, but if I do my job correctly, this will run very smoothly with only minimal input from me. Ideally the group is the star of the show. The aim is for

us to share our desires as they relate to what we wish to create in the world, in a judgment free, collaborative and inclusive space."

- I continue with, "The Code of Conduct is as follows: be kind and considerate, play full out, take notes, keep an open mind, and don't sugar-coat. Confidentiality is a must. Do not share anything outside the group without full consent of the person who shared."

## AGAIN, BE A GREAT LEADER

In order to become a great mastermind leader, you also have to embody a great mastermind member to be a great example for your members. We need to take ultimate responsibility to make sure that any group that we participate in or facilitate is a smashing success for all concerned. *Extreme Ownership*[2] is a great book to check out if you haven't already, if you really want to go down the rabbit hole of principled and effective leadership. It's the best book I've read on the topic in the last five years.

---

[2] *Extreme Ownership: How U.S. Navy SEALs Lead and Win* by Jocko Willink (see photo) and Leif Babin (St. Martin's Press, 2017)

*Me with* Extreme Ownership *author, Jocko Willink*

Here are the traits and habits that make a mastermind participant great (feel free to work these into the code of conduct for your mastermind):

- **Always seek to give first.** Remember, the law of reciprocity is one of the core laws of influence, and it works at every single level of play in this game called life. When you give wholeheartedly, it opens you up for receiving wholeheartedly. But you must give first without reservation. People are very attuned to knowing when someone is just giving to get or holding back. They can't always articulate it, but they can feel it and will do the same consciously or unconsciously in return.

- **Respect others and yourself.** If you don't give respect to yourself and others, how can you expect them to respect you? On the flip side, not taking anything personally will serve you incredibly well in this type of environment. People are delving into their most difficult areas of life. Their baggage will come up and they will get triggered. In this state, they may say and do things that don't align with your highest vision of them or their highest identity for themselves. Don't take it personally, and definitely don't let their behavior rain on your parade. It's likely a stress reaction and has nothing to do with you. Remember, everyone is fighting a battle that you know nothing about, and there are only two types of communication: a loving response and a cry for help. Don't take cries for help personally, just help!

- **Have great boundaries.** When you are truly healthy, you have great boundaries and communication around those boundaries. You don't create expectations, you create agreements, and clearly communicate in a calm and professional manner what acceptable and unacceptable behavior is. You can be playful as well with this, no need to take it personally or get uptight about it. People again will push your buttons sometimes, master the skill of gently guiding them back on the path to the light. If they really continue to trample on your clearly defined agreements and boundaries that have been communicated effectively, give them warning, then cut them off if they persist. Ain't nobody got time for that. It's okay to fire a client or stop helping someone if they simply won't work with you for mutual benefit. It's in their own best interest to do so, after all! But always remember the ABCs of interpersonal dealings: Create **A**greements, not expectations. Set clear **B**oundaries and give people a second chance if they make an honest mistake with positive intent. And finally, don't forget to **C**ommunicate at every interval along the way.

- **Be impeccable with your word**. If you say you are going to do something, do it. Right then and there is the ideal scenario, or at least take the first step if it's more involved and can't be done then. If that's just putting it in the calendar for the next time you CAN do it, then that's the action to do right now. It's not real until it's booked in the calendar. If something comes up outside your control that means you can't do something as you first promised, make sure to clearly communicate that as soon as you can, and make it up to that person asap. If you break your word, you lose commitment and consistency, which loses trust, and that is NOT the mark of a leader that people can follow, and will quickly begin to pull away, which can undermine relationships with others as well. So keep your word, take action right now, and always seek to overdeliver. In fact, you can use what I call the 200%

rule: Promise 90% less and deliver 110% of what you promise. You can never go wrong.

- **No pitching**. There is a time and a place for pitching, and it's when you have rapport, trust, and comfort built. It's also when you've asked people for permission to pitch them. This isn't usually during a mastermind, so be mindful of when you or others get into pitch mode and gently guide them back to open communication and solving one another's challenges.

- **Keep time sacred and don't run over**. As facilitator of a paid mastermind, you must have two things, a note taker and a time keeper. These can be the same person if they're talented, but it can just as easily be two people. The time keeper should call it at the halfway point, the two-minutes-left mark, and when the last share is taking place. They can also do double duty, calling on people as they raise their hands to share or ask questions, depending on where you are in the cycle.

- **Have some forethought and clarity going in**. As a participant, you can be so much more efficient with time if you know what you are going to say going in to the challenge portion of the hot seat. Taking even 3-5 minutes to jot down some bullet points will save you so much time in clarifying questions and give you much more time for solutions because you can get to the heart of the problem that much quicker.

- **Be humble and grateful**. People can't stand a person who either brags all the time or isn't grateful. Don't be that person. If you have trouble finding things to be grateful for, watch some documentaries and shows about how most of the world lives, or give your time to organizations that feed, clothe and provide shelter for those in need. You need more contrast to understand just how blessed you are and how good most of us truly have it. If you really don't understand or resonate with how good life is in 2019, then you really need to study history more. This is by far the best ever time in history to be alive.

- **Take action**. Take action. Form habits. Gain momentum. DO NOT STOP. Enough said.

- **Be accountable for yourself and others**. You are a leader now and being a leader means seeking to provide clarity, accountability and support to yourself and others in every possible circumstance.

- **Give trust to get it**. You must be willing to give what you want to get. If you want people to open up, you must be willing to be vulnerable first. If you want people to take action, you must raise the standard first. If you want people to be great clients, you must yourself be a great client. If you want people to invest, you must invest in yourself. YOU MUST BE WILLING TO GIVE THAT WHICH YOU WANT TO RECEIVE. It is only in giving that we can gain what we truly want, need and desire.

# 5. RUN YOUR

# MEETING

"A problem well defined is half solved."
—CHARLES KETTERING

# AMBER TACY

I MET BRAD for lunch at a small cafe in NYC one afternoon, just to catch up. After some chitchat, Brad asked the simple "So, how *are* you?" And if you know Brad you'll know that the usual "Oh, fine." never flies. Brad has this unique ability to pull out the big stuff. The real stuff. I began to express how stressed I was in my everyday life. The root of this stress fell on my financial concerns. My business was struggling. Although we had just met for lunch and to catch up, Brad heard me and, in the most genuine way, responded with, "I think I have a way to help."

It's been eight weeks with MMM. And I'm not exaggerating when I say my business has been more successful and grown more in the last eight weeks than in the last eight months. The strategic planning, unlimited resources, the network, the personalized mentorship. These are a few ways that MMM has ensured my greatness. But it's the unmatched support from this team and from the other members that has given me the confidence boost I needed to take my business to the next level. They have not only helped me to set the bar high, but they have taken away every barrier and insecurity I might encounter, making success inevitable.

Had I not followed through and joined MMM after my lunch with Brad, I would still have a "hobby" instead of a business. The stress I would feel burdened with would be crippling. The confidence I have because of this team and knowing they will not let me fail is unparalleled. If you're fine where you're at, if you're comfortable with your business or your job, if you're not interested in personal growth and building deep, meaningful relationships with people who will literally dance over your smallest victories, you need not apply. But should you be interested in doubling your rates, moving forward without fear of failure, or should you want to Make More Marbles, I encourage you to reach out to Brad and his team.

As a young and ambitious entrepreneur, working with Brad Hart was one of the best things I have ever done. He is an incredible relationship builder, having connections with some of the top leaders in online marketing, eCommerce, and beyond. He supports people with the opportunities and education they need to succeed in whatever capacity is best for them. He also has a "bam-bam-bam" work style. He gets things done. If you are looking to rapidly and effectively enter the world of someone who is doing big things and who will support you in achieving your own dreams, I highly recommend getting into Brads circle.

—Amber Tacy

# GET THE BALL ROLLING

SOMETIMES BEING KIND is not about being nice or coddling someone, it's helping people come to the right awareness level to make the shift that's sometimes obvious to everyone, except them, AND being able to do that with the patience, grace, compassion and understanding that we would all expect from the members of such a high vibration community, *which is what you're creating!* Building upon what we've discussed about leadership, two fun acronyms to start us off are SEEDS and CROPS:

- SEEDS: Seek in Every Encounter to Diagnose, create Space, Serve, Support and Solve.
- CROPS: Connect them to Resources, Opportunities, People, Systems that will help them further their mission faster.

By now you've explained the format for newbies. Have the first person (or two) be someone who has gone before. Set a timer for 8 minutes and get into it! As the facilitator, here are some fun questions to get the ball rolling:

- (If the person is new) "In 30 seconds, what's your name, and who do you serve?"
- "In 30 seconds, what are you celebrating or grateful for right now?"
- "In 60 seconds, what is your biggest challenge right now in life or business, or what is something you want to move faster on?"
- "How can we best support you right now?"

And you're rolling! *Don't* jump right into solutions, but spend a couple minutes probing deeper. Ask clarifying questions. (I've supplied a great resource of questions later in this book.) Then clarify and verify that everyone is on the same page with what the problem or challenge is. When everyone present is clear on the problem, solutions are natural and easy. If you DON'T actually get clarity, then you will have a hard time moving forward with success and results will not be complete and long-lasting.

A problem well-stated and understood is half-solved. Usually you'll notice that the answer comes out in the questioning process, but if you're not clear on what the problem IS, it's exceptionally difficult to solve it, as you end up adding further complexity or solving a problem that's adjacent or only a symptom, but not the actual root cause.

Keep suggestions tight and to the point. If elaboration is needed, set up a sidebar for after the meeting. Don't hog time, just be efficient and tell them what you've got. Don't devolve into a coaching session just to hear yourself speak, and make sure other members refrain from this as well. I help keep the group focused and make sure that everyone has their share of time. It's more important to get clear, THEN we overwhelm the problem with possible solutions. And if out of time this can take the form of, "Hey, come see me after, I have something for that," or "Hey, I know exactly who you should talk to next, let me make an introduction afterward," or something of that nature.

Challenges and Celebrations: It's okay to share wins, celebrations, and gratitude as well! We're not always plagued by challenges, and I certainly don't invite that as the only possibility. But we do ask that you hold yourself accountable to bringing to the space whatever you would like the collective time, energy, and attention of the group to be focused on. Sometimes things are going great and you just want to create even MORE momentum!

Promises: When you make a promise to someone in the space, write it down and take an action right then to either complete the loop or at least get the ball rolling, putting it in the calendar with an invite to that person to follow up. Whatever you promise might be minor or trivial to you, but could very possibly change the game for them, so creating agreements, not expectations, and follow-through is key. Doing so will create specific, considerate, immediate value for another human being.

Examples include but are not limited to:

- Holding space
- An ear to listen
- Emotional support
- Fun, a joke, something silly
- A connection
- A resource

- A book (or a quick synopsis)
- An opportunity
- A system or tool they could use
- An event they could attend
- A course they could take
- A group, tribe or mastermind they could join
- A mentor to connect them with
- A rock star service provider they need
- A trip or travel they could go on
- A person who would change their life

This is how you develop relationships with people and help them. No strings attached. No expectation. No waiting for the other shoe to drop. Show them who you are, an abundant individual, and add value without reservation. You'll be SHOCKED at how this comes back to you in waves. Especially if you're operating from a place of service and gratitude. If you are ready to give and receive in abundance it will literally come back to you 20x of what you put out (but I'm probably preaching to the choir here).

Also, we all sell things. To sell is human, but please do not sell to this group in the container we are creating. If someone raises their hand and says, "Hey, I want to have a chat about what you offer," by all means, create a follow-up discussion for after the group meeting but let's keep this group focused on masterminding, not on selling our wonderful products and services to one another.

Cool? Cool.

These principles are the basis of any great mastermind and can be included in letters to your members about the process.

When it's time to move on, you must. People will always be yapping, so be sure to say "last share" when you're at the one-minute left mark. Also, in the beginning, make sure people keep it tight (30 seconds) on who they are and what they do, as well as celebrations and gratitude. The challenge might take a little longer to describe, but you can prompt them to be concise with questions like: "What's the main challenge right now?" Or if they're rambling, simply put up your hand and sum up what they said in a sentence.

At the end of their share and time, I like to check in and ask a golden question: "Do you feel supported right now?" I've now asked this question thousands of times and almost nobody ever says no. But if they DO say no, that's an opportunity to drop in with that person afterward and make sure they get what they need—whether connections, resources, opportunities, etc. But people almost always answer yes. You can't help but feel that way when all eyes are on you and everyone in the room is pulling for you.

Rinse and repeat until everyone has gotten a chance to go or you run out of time! Leaders go last, so don't mastermind yourself until the end. I normally don't unless people ask me to or I have a really pressing challenge I need input on and support with.

Keep the sales pitches out and keep the asks short. This is not a pitch fest (for you or others).

# THE ICEBERG
# ANALOGY

I WANT TO use a fun analogy to describe the process of how people move along their clarity journey and ultimately can see what they didn't see before, so you, the facilitator can easily see where they're at and where they still need to go. First, the person on the hot seat comes along and they have their presenting problem (or PP for short). This PP is just the tip of the iceberg. If you've ever seen an iceberg in real life, or even watched the movie Titanic, you probably know that 10 percent of the iceberg is what's above water, and 90 percent of the iceberg is below the frigid waters. It might even be nice and sunny on top of that iceberg. It might be safe and warm. They might have built an igloo and be hanging out with some penguins and seals and stuff. But we all know now that the problems people present to us are rarely the whole problem, or the root of the problem. Sometimes up to 90 percent of the problem is truly under the surface.

Another way to look at this is the idea that we only use 10 percent of our brains at any given time. This is actually true, but it's out of context in which it really goes. You DO use 100 percent of your brain, but you only use 10 percent of your brain CONSCIOUSLY. The rest are subconscious processes like breathing, fight or flight, sleeping, repairing, digesting, and all the other things that your body gratefully does without you having to think about it. This also—and here's where this ties in—includes filters like generalizations, distortions, and deletions. This includes possible traumas that are locked down memory-wise and you don't know why you're triggered by what can be a very easy problem for someone else to move through, etc. So just like the iceberg is actually 90 percent under the surface, we have to get clarity by asking clarifying questions until we can clearly see the whole iceberg. And people go through phases when this is happening that I'll share with you now.

The first step is they have a challenge which they are willing to confess. Without this, we can't go any deeper. You won't believe how many times I've had people try to defer on their hot seat saying, "Everything is great right now!" or "My challenges are no big deal!" And they're trying to be deferential to the group and allow them to get the time that they need. Most of this can be chalked up to worthiness issues or sometimes ego. Usually what we've found after literally thousands of iterations is once you get this person talking, there's definitely a challenge or at least something that is stalled or slowed down that they want to move faster on. *So keep on people. Get them talking. Leadership is intrusive and uncomfortable, because all growth happens outside your comfort zone.* At least get them to share their name, what they're up to in the world, and what they're grateful for or celebrating right now. That will at least get them talking and build rapport so that you can easily transition into what's actually going on.

I'll also tease them and say something like, "So your challenge if I'm hearing you correctly is that you have no challenges and are bored? How can we add some exciting problems so this (gentleman, lady) has some worthy opponents in his/her life?" Or I kindly rib them that I'll gladly give them one of my challenges to solve if they really have nothing going on. Usually this is enough to get them talking, but if someone really doesn't want to share, you also don't want to push too far and waste the group's time, so just make a note to follow up after with them privately, make sure everything is actually alright, and then move along.

The step after stating the PP or the challenge and being willing to confess it to the group is the most interesting to navigate. It's the confusion that enters. Now, you're off of the tip of the iceberg and in the freezing cold waters of Confusion. This is where clarifying questions are so key, because they'll help people chunk up or chunk down as needed in order to gain outside perspective on the challenge and get to the heart of what's actually going on in the clear light of day. When clarity is achieved, you can now see the whole iceberg for what it really is. It's just a big chunk of frozen water. No big deal.

## ADVANCED FACILITATING

Now that you have clarity, you can begin to conspire with the group to fill in the rest of what you need to solve that problem, summed in another handy acronym, CASTLE. This is some advanced stuff for facilitators.

The intention for each mastermind meetup is *co-creation*. We want a space where conscious co-creators (entrepreneurs) can come together and collaborate, creating more for everyone instead of just competing with one another. We want members helping one another crush challenges and achieving their goals through the CASTLE of characters they show up as:

- Clarity
- Accountability
- Support
- Trust
- Leverage
- Engagement

Or if we're keeping with the Cs alliteration:

- Clarity
- Conspiring and co-creation
- Commitment
- Community support
- Consequences if the plan is not executed by a certain date.

You get the idea. You'll create a clear, step-by-step action plan which can look something like this, as you flesh it out:

**Problem:**

- I'm not getting enough leads for my business and revenues are down.

**Potential solutions:**

- Spend more money on advertising.
- Create more content and publish on more channels with a strong message and call to action.
- Ask your current customer base for referrals which you pay them for.
- Run a promotion or sale to drive more business.

- Ask potential referral partners to promote in exchange for an affiliate commission.

*SOLUTIONS are only valid once we have CLARITY on the real problem, so do NOT skip the clarifying questions phase.*

Once the person has clarity on what the real problem is, and they have potential solutions, the next step is to create a container where they can truly achieve and accomplish the thing. This is where ongoing community support is so important. Most people are men/women of their words, but when there's money on the line and consequences more than just saving face, more gets done faster which builds the execution muscles and that's what's needed most. Not what's easy, not what's convenient, not drifting from one thing to the next, but consistent, massive action. If the action they are taking is not getting the desired result, they switch to one of the many other solutions that are available. For example, the largest amount of money someone has put down is $3,000 and you better believe they got it done because they definitely did NOT want to lose the money. It works at any level, given the financial commitment is big enough to make them uncomfortable and they have given their word to the group.

Finally, and this is key, because it's happened to me in the past, you'll find something that works and then not keep doing it. The habit you want to form as soon as something works in a business is to systematize it by creating a video walkthrough, a workflow, and a checklist. Now this is a thing you can either automate or hire out to do and then set up performance incentives for it to get done with checks and balances in the form of reports and reviews. Otherwise the likelihood that the thing is going to keep getting done and the result is going to keep getting achieved is slim to nil. The best way to get something done is the mechanize it and make sure someone is paid to always be feeding that machine, with regular checks and balances in place along the way at specified (and sometimes surprise) intervals where there is a reporting and reviewing structure in place.

That in a nutshell is how you go through the entire cycle, from challenge to a clear committed process that makes sure the problem stays solved for good.

And if it's not broken, you don't have to fix it.

The whole goal in business is to get off the time-for-money wheel as soon as humanly possible and get a machine in place to add value to the marketplace in exchange for money whether you're there to turn the crank or feed the machine or not. That's how you become an owner, not an operator. That's how you start having the ability to work ON the business and not IN the business. You are no longer a bottleneck through which anything needs to pass or any cog in any part of it. You, as Tim Ferriss so elegantly put it in the *4-Hour Workweek*, are simply a cop on the side of the road. You can step in and handle something as needed, but mostly you're just letting the traffic go by And making sure the money is still piling up as intended. Your job becomes more of a diagnostician/problem solver, and that's the most valuable skill in business.

People who can accurately diagnose and solve problems are the very best mastermind leaders and the most valuable people in any business, period. Anyone can do the work once the process is figured out to get the results reliably. The real genius is seeing what others don't and being able to transform a problem that people have into an opportunity for continued value addition to the marketplace, which equals revenue generated which equals potential impact across all areas of life. The mastermind is just one more way to sharpen your skill set, which in my opinion is the number one skill set that everyone should seek to hone to the very best of their ability until they're world-class.

Using this process you can literally solve any problem that shows up in life.

We've had people in our masterminds come through with every single type of issue you can imagine—health challenges, relationship challenges, business challenges, personal challenges, spiritual challenges. You can't even imagine the types of shifts that people get using this simple but powerful framework.

It never fails to work if you work it.

If people are having some resistance in the beginning to masterminding, or just genuinely unsure what to focus on in their lives, here's what I recommend starting out with. There's an incredible exercise called the Wheel of Life which can be an invaluable way of getting clarity on what area of your life you have the most challenges in right now. It's simple, you just draw a circle, and then pick the following categories and make slices through the circle so each one is a wedge. Then you label them:

- Health
- Business
- Finances
- Relationships
- Spirituality
- Giving

And you begin to ask yourself without judgment how you feel about each area in turn and assign it a 1 being totally awful to a 10 being a slam-dunk and everything is legitimately outstanding. Then, as you look around the wheel that you've now created it will begin to become very clear that you can go slow with this wheel or deal with the bumps, but if you wanted to go fast and start really getting after it, one of these areas is a bump in the wheel that's going to make it fly off and you're going to crash. The solution is to simply focus on the area where you need the greatest improvement and use that as a starting point on a challenge.

I've had complete atheists with no respect for God, religion or any tradition come along and realize that spirituality was their weakest place in life. Now granted, they were willing to commit and admit that they would like more in that particular area and were willing to work on it with the group and gain their actionable advice and insights, and that's what he got—a tailor-made plan for him to develop his own relationship with the divine, as it made sense to him.

It's not about knowing exactly what you're going to get, gently remind people, it's about being open to whatever might show up when we are receptive and we work the process. It really does work when you work it.

I'm so endlessly grateful to be able to share this with you so you can now go off and use it to solve any problem in your life, or really, any problem in the world. And if you're ever feeling overwhelmed, remember, *clarity is the key to everything.*

# QUESTIONS FOR FACILITATORS

ASK CLARIFYING QUESTIONS. Clarify and verify that everyone is on the same page as to what the problem or challenge is. Be cognizant when people start to drift off topic or segue inappropriately. There are three types of questions to ask:

1. *Chunking up* questions in order to zoom out and see the bigger picture,
2. *Chunking down* questions in order to zoom in,
3. *Segue* questions to change the topic entirely.

Usually people ask segue questions when they are uncomfortable themselves with the line of inquiry. In other words, someone else is in the hot seat, and they are about to have a breakthrough and get really clear on the true nature of their challenge, but it makes someone else in the room uncomfortable. When this happens, you must notice it with your sensory acuity and gently remind people to stay on topic, chunking down/drilling down until you hit pay dirt.

Remember, CLARITY is the number one most important thing in the mastermind. When everyone present is clear on the problem, then solutions are natural and easy. Unless there's a lot of time left after the clarity portion, it's rare that all solutions can be presented in the time allotted. Remember, this is a free mastermind setting, not a deep dive. The number one goal is clarity, anything else is a bonus. After that, people can put accountability and support structures into place on their own time. This is why I limit hot seats to 10-12 and the total group size to 20, because otherwise we drift. If people are verbose remind them that we only have a limited time and we need to keep moving, but you have an hour afterward for general networking and to propose additional solutions. Make a note and follow up with that person afterward.

This works best when everyone has seen it play through two or three times, and don't worry, people won't "get it" at first. That's natural. Just gently remind them to keep an open mind, and they'll quickly see how powerful this framework is for destroying problems in their tracks.

Optional: You can place bets with people that they will accomplish a task by a certain date. They put up an amount of money (other people can add to the kitty as well to cheer them on) that will motivate them not to lose the bet. If they win, they get all the money back. If they lose, the money goes to a charity that can be voted on by the mastermind membership. Suggest three options as leader and take a FB poll to set that standard.

This really works but can be sticky and tricky to manage, so I wouldn't consider doing this until you've been running the mastermind at least six months consistently and people know you, like you, and trust you not to skip with their money. Or you could simply not take their money, but it's way more effective when held in escrow. The biggest bet so far someone has made is $3,000 and they completed it. Most bets range $500-$1,000. The amount is only relevant in comparison to how much it would suck for that person to lose it. Rich people should bet more. I've had people bet their rent money, but damn Skippy if they didn't deliver on their promise to themselves. Worst case, they learn a lesson, and a charity gets a nice donation to help move their mission forward faster.

## GREAT QUESTIONS TO ASK AS A LEADER

Sometimes it's on you as the leader to make sure that:

- People participate by asking questions and suggesting solutions,
- The questions are thoughtful and relevant and help people either chunk up to see the bigger picture or chunk down into detail for clarity.
- Don't segue off-topic for no reason.

Here are some examples you can use:

- "Tell us more about that."
- "What would life look like if this was solved?"
- "Has anyone else ever experienced X?" This is a great one to show people they are not alone in their struggle.
- "Who would be the perfect person to solve this?"
- "What's great about this challenge?"
- "Who would you need to be for this to be a piece of cake?"
- "Does this show up anywhere else in your life?"
- "Tell us what you've tried so far."

You'll know you've asked a great question when the energy shifts in a person's body, or the room lights up with pleasant sounds from the person on the hot seat or the other participants in the room.

## META QUESTIONS

A *meta question* is a "question about a question." They're not used to avoid but to gain clarity.

- "If I could make this work, how would I?"
- "What's great about this?"
- "What if I did know the answer right now?"
- "What is this costing you?"
- "What would life or business look like if this problem was solved?"
- "What challenges might come up in the future as you execute that we can solve now as well?"
- "What's the one challenge, that if solved, would make all other challenges lesser or irrelevant?"
- "What's the one thing that if you focused on it, would go the farthest and cause the most good?"
- "Since you know yourself better than anyone else, what tools, resources and support would you need to make this a reality?"
- "What's a surprising way that you could attack this problem?" (Shock and awe.)
- "Do you feel supported right now?"
- "Who are the people in your life that might be disincentivized to support you?" (Secondary benefits, etc.)
- "If you succeed, who wins and who loses? How can you make it a win-win-win all around?"

- "What are the elements of your environment that need to shift in order to support your best habits most consistently?"
- "If you could wave a magic wand and fix any problem in your life or business, what would it be?"
- The Five Whys: "What's most important to you? What's important to you about that? What does that give you?" Each using the NLP questions framework:
  o Freedom
  o Love
  o Inner peace
  o Happiness
  o Fulfillment
- Ultimate Perfect Future: "What do you want to achieve in your lifetime, regardless of whether it's currently possible or not?"
- "Has anyone ever dealt with this before? Raise your hand if you've ever dealt with this before."
- "If one of your successful experiences could be relevant to this challenge, what could it possibly be?"

## NOT-SELF QUESTIONS

- "What's really going on?"
- "What are you afraid of?"
- "What are you trying to prove? To whom?"
- "What does this mean to you? What could it mean?"
- "What do you have to let go of in order to get to the next level? Even if—or especially if—it's gotten you where you are, but will get you no further?"
- "Are you trying to convince everyone that you are certain?"
- "Are you avoiding confrontation, or truth?"
- "Are you holding onto something that isn't good for you?"

- "Are you in a hurry to get things done simply so you can be free of the pressure?"
- "Are you trying to answer everybody else's questions?"

## LETTING GO QUESTIONS (By Hale Dwoskin)

- "Welcome what you are feeling right now."
- "Can you let this go?"
- "Would you?"
- "When?"

## FEAR-SETTING QUESTIONS (By Tim Ferriss)

- "What is the absolute worst thing that could happen?"
- "How would you come back?"
- "How can you limit the risks?"
- "What is the best case scenario?"

## SAVAGE QUESTIONS (Use sparingly!)

- "Are you happy with the results of your life so far?"
- "Are you comfortable with relying on this style of operating your business?"
- "Who's fault is it that you don't have what you want in your life?"
- "How committed to your vision are you? Scale of one to ten?"
- "What has to happen for you to get out of your own way?"
- "Are you ready to make a new decision?"
- "When is right now the time to change your mind?"
- "Can you imagine the impact that this decision will have? How else?"

- "How open minded are you about talking about _____?"
- "Just out of curiosity… What needs to happen for you to make a decision about this?"
- "What is stopping you from moving forward with this right now?"
- "Can you imagine your life with/without this?"
- "Who are you letting down by not stepping up?"
- "What makes you say that?"
- "How would you feel if this decision was the key turning point? If your competition passed you? If you turned this around? If you lost everything?"

## ADDITIONAL COACHING QUESTIONS:

- "How do you see your mission or vision manifesting currently?"
- If multiple: "Which of these lights you up more when you envision it?"
- "How informed do you feel about taking the next necessary steps?"
- When clear on the next steps: "How excited do you feel on a scale of 1-10 about taking these next actions?"
- If not excited: "What else do you still need clarity on to feel completely aligned and ready for action?"
- "What additional tools, resources and support do you need?"
- "How can you stay committed and accountable to your vision and keep taking action?"

## WHEN ENCOUNTERING RESISTANCE (With credit to Michael Hazen and Jessie Medina)

- "Am what I'm attached to worth the stubbornness?"

- "Am I being blind to another area of my life?"
- "Is this a chance for persistence and leveling up? And/or innovation that comes when I slow down?"
- "What's the worst that could happen if I set this down?"
- "Does it pose a real threat to me or my family's well-being?"
- "Am I walking in my divine purpose?"
- "Am I playing small or feeling like an impostor?"
- "Am I aligned with what I'm really supposed to be doing?"
- "Am I willing to change courses even if it seems crazy or others wouldn't get it at first?"
- "Am I willing to be authentic and transparent to myself?"

## CUSTOMER ANALYSIS AND AUDIENCE SEGMENTATION QUESTIONS (Inspired by Karyn Greenstreet)

- "Who do you want to serve, overall?"
- "Do any of these potential clients fall into buckets?"
- "Which ones DON'T you want to work with anymore?"
- "Is there a NEW audience you want to serve?"
- "What keeps them up at night? What problems do they want to solve?"
- "Which practical, concrete results do your members want?"
- "What does their ultimate perfect future look like?" (Gives you a North Star.)
- "What emotions do they want to feel on a regular basis? How do they want to feel during and after your mastermind group?"

- "Does your audience know what a mastermind group is? If not, how will you explain how it works to them with benefits driven languaging in 1-3 sentences?"

# TROUBLE-SHOOTING

## JERKS

- Kick them out and disinvite them. One bad apple spoils the bunch. People get exactly one chance to course correct, otherwise, ain't nobody got time for that.

## PEOPLE NOT ON FACEBOOK

- Have them partner up with someone who IS on Facebook to get details and information about meetings and the group as needed.

## HANGERS ON IN PUBLIC SPACES

- Invite them in! Why not? If there's time, have them mastermind and experience the magic for themselves. Give them the ground rules and explain that even if they don't get it, the number one rule is privacy and not to repeat anything to anyone outside the space without their consent.

# DISCOVER THE PODCAST!

Want to hear ME run MY mastermind and get a ton of value from the hot seats while you're at it? Check out the *8-Minute Mastermind Podcast* (Don't forget to rate, subscribe, and share if you like it!).

https://makemoremarbles.com/podcasts/

# 6. END A MEETING

# STEPHEN VETTER

WHAT A RESONATING newsletter. After our mastermind last week, I have been making small tweaks to put myself back in my flow state. Yesterday my truck got broken into and damaged (I have it lined up to be sold today), I was grateful that instead of finding frustration, or panic, I just laughed out loud, and went immediately to work on how to create a solution within the timeline so I would still be able to sell it in great condition.

That is a testament to the personal growth I have done and added fuel to the fire of finding my harmonious rhythm with my world. This morning was the real kicker though, listening to a podcast with Tony Robbins and Gary Vaynerchuk I had a realization that I lost my flow state not by changing my actions, but by changing my attitude towards my actions. I had lost connection to focusing on "what value am I adding?" and reverted to "what action am I doing?"

I went immediately to life thresholds and how I have been working on finding the next threshold. What I failed to acknowledge until this morning is that when entering a new threshold, I am now again at the bottom of a new level, and what I have been experiencing is not regression, but progression into a new threshold where I am now again at the bottom with an exciting and new climb ahead of me.

I attribute THAT to masterminding, and surrounding myself with loving and supportive people, like yourself, and other mentors. This newsletter very much embedded that and today I am extremely grateful for you, your newsletters, the MMM Mastermind, and the RE-recognizing that it is all about the attitude towards the actions, asking the right questions, and always seeking first to understand, and focus on "what is the value that I can add?"

—STEPHEN VETTER

# ...BUT YOU CAN'T STAY HERE.

DURING THE NETWORKING time, make sure people know what time they are expected to leave (especially if it's in your home and you have a strict bedtime, otherwise people will hang out forever). This way, if it starts getting toward that time, it's easy to say, "Hey gang, it's just about that time, you don't have to go home, but you can't stay here."

If people are new, during the networking time, I'll make it a point to make sure I have their contact info and ask them if they enjoyed it and if they would come back again. I've never had anyone say no. The compliments are endless, and a little embarrassing sometimes, but these breakthroughs make all the difference to that person, so never underestimate the amount of value this mastermind group can add to their lives. It's really a magical experience that I'm incredibly grateful to be able to share with you in this book and with the free 21-day challenge:

www.buildamastermind.com/challenge

It pays to check in with people, get everyone's phone number at the end, thank them for coming individually at the end. Ask them about their experience, and if they would come again when the mastermind is finished. Make sure that if you make a promise, you keep it (the 200% rule—promise 90% less and deliver 110%) and always, ALWAYS communicate when circumstances outside your control dictate that you cannot. Introductions should always be made double opt-in and with consent of both parties.

Make sure they know WHAT'S NEXT—when the *next* mastermind is taking place, for example—and remind them to take massive action and follow their prescriptions from the meetup, etc.

Finally, make sure to take a photo of the entire group and post it in the Facebook group! Selfies (ussies?) work best.

# 7. SCALE!

"I have three rules, help a lot of people, have a lot of fun, make a lot of money."

—Dave Meltzer

# BRIAN FOUTS

WHEN I FIRST met Brad, it was with a group of other high achievers, like a summer camp for entrepreneurs. This was a great group and Brad fit in very well. My brother Jake and I had a successful financial education business and we were generating consistently mid-five figures of revenue per month. I was looking for a way to scale and level up the business, but I wasn't exactly sure what our next step was. Despite our initial success, I didn't feel satisfied in my business and I knew we could change the financial destinies of more people. So I was keeping an open mind for a person to work with and provide some additional resources, direction, and vision for my business. I didn't know it at the time, but Brad Hart was that person.

Soon after meeting Brad, I joined his mastermind because I immediately recognized the value of being plugged in with a highly successful, growth-oriented community. Brad's ability to diagnose problems, find solutions, and create massive value quickly is by far the best I've experienced in all my entrepreneurial career. After being aligned with Brad for less than two months, a very lucrative opportunity arose to work with him and I jumped right in. By working with Brad for a mere two months, we created a course launch that made over $50,000 in our first three days during our beta test. Our business suddenly had access to higher level input and strategies, as well as resources that helped us look at how to move into 2018 with a better plan and a greater vision of what's possible.

By having access to Brad and his team, a plethora of effective strategies, and the high mindedness of an entrepreneurial community, my revenue has increased, my costs have decreased, and I'm able to maximize some of our current resources, which has added to our bottom line. Ultimately, working with Brad has impacted the most important people in any business—our clients. Our clients are better served because we are able to deliver better and higher quality content on a larger scale so that they can financially transform their lives.

I would strongly recommend working with Brad if you are looking to grow your business, especially if you feel stuck or unsure of what steps to take to break through the ceiling. The choice to work with Brad has been an absolute no-brainer, as I have already 3x my initial investment in one weekend!

And we're just getting started.

—BRIAN FOUTS

# THE NUMBER ONE WORD IN AN ENTREPRENEUR'S VOCABULARY

WHILE EVERYONE IS going for scale, you're scaling up your impact with the right people. "Scale" is currently the number one word in an entrepreneur's vocabulary. You've heard the old saying, "Nail it, then scale it." And this is true. You've gotta put in the hours, the blood, sweat, and tears to really be sure that your product or service is actually a hit. And the only way to really make money nowadays is to serve more people more efficiently. But what does this cost along the way? What if we can scale up our impact, with the right individuals, and make sure that we're investing in the right leaders?

Now, I believe that everyone holds within them the potential for greatness. But greatness comes at a steep price— one of discipline, consistency, and commitment that most will never muster and therefore most potential will remain just that—untapped *potential*. It's a sad truth. Some people just want it more and they're willing to work hard and smart until they get it. In any group of people there are between 1 and 5 percent AT MOST who will actually do the work and reap the rewards worth talking about.

There are no shortcuts.

So as a speaker, coach, consultant: the type of entrepreneur who works in some way to mentor people and help them achieve results, you MUST be discerning in the vehicles you choose. And it's okay to use multiple vehicles to get multiple types of results. Once you've nailed and scaled your core offer, it makes sense to have a higher-end offer for those select few who are really going to win and stand out. They've already shown up and done the work, either with you or others. They are coachable. They are people who believe in investing in themselves to gain slight edges wherever they can. They are the people with whom all you need to do is throw a little rocket fuel on their already burning fire, and they're going to blast off in the ways that most people just won't. This is why having a *paid mastermind offer* is CRUCIAL if you want to scale. It will give you the lab, the place to experiment, figure out what works, and create new offerings.

But not just that, it allows you to go DEEP with the RIGHT people, and for an investment that really gets you revved-up and ready to give every single thing you've got. And give you should—everything at your disposal—all content, all workflows, all tools, all access to the network (provided it adds value to the those you're introducing to as well). Because this is the place to create the biggest breakthroughs for your clients, to hold nothing back and really turn the volume knob up to

11. The mastermind is the place where you make certain they get a 10X result in their lives and business compared to what they pay. Go for 100X if you can manage it.

That gives you not only the juice and fulfillment in knowing that you can really blow the doors off for people (like adding $200k to their business in three months and making $50k weeks a regular occurrence), but that you can take that into almost any organization at any level and shine. And you'll have the testimonials to open those doors and overcome those objections so when people make a decision, you can be congruent in helping them make the best decision because you KNOW THAT WHAT YOU DO WORKS.

Yes, there will be resistance. Yes, you will learn. This never stops. Life doesn't get easier, you get better. So focus, be disciplined, and blow the doors off for people however you possibly can:

- Connections
- Resources
- Opportunities
- People
- Systems

If you don't have the answer, who does? For whom would this problem be child's play? How can they afford it? Can you work a deal on their behalf based on your relationship? There are so many ways to solve a problem. It all starts with clarity, then commit to solving it and never give up until it's solved. It's a simple formula, but not easy. Which is why training is SO important. You must train and steel your mind every single day until whatever shows up becomes child's play. But potential energy will never make a car go. It must be converted into kinetic energy. Masterminds are the vehicle to do this with your top clients. Period. Of all the models—1:1, group coaching, webinars—it has the HIGHEST impact and the BEST ROI of time, money, energy and attention.

HAVE A BIG HEART AND A TALL FENCE. Not everyone is deserving of you at your best. They've got to be in a place where that makes sense. It's just the hard truth. *If you give too much to the wrong people, you'll constantly feel like a martyr and will not end up having enough energy to give your best to the right people.* You can't help someone if they're not in a position to be helped. And because you have a big heart and a tall fence, you can devote your energy where it gains the biggest ROI. That's really a key skill to master in life, creating vehicles through which to serve that allow you to dedicate your gifts in the highest ROI way. And it's from that space of abundance that you then create, giving wholeheartedly and holding nothing of yourself back. Because YOUR needs are met, your capacity expands geometrically.

So in the conversation of scale, once you have your core offer and people are getting after it, pay attention to your top performers who demonstrate the best mindset and results. Create your mastermind offer to blast those people off. Don't settle for anything less than what they were born to give, be, do, and have. And in doing so, set yourself up to HAVE to step up to give the same. When you are in that flow, giving all of yourself that you possibly can, magic happens.

Whether you believe in divinity, God, the universe, what have you, some higher power is always working in your life. This is how regular humans do superhuman things that cannot be explained. You don't have to wait around for the scientific answer to tap into that flow. You simply DECIDE, COMMIT and TAKE ACTION. This is true of all areas of life. If you are going your hardest, you are giving everything you've got, you will be given more. If you half-ass it, everything will slowly be taken from you in each area of life.

And when you are showing up as a leader, in your highest and best possible self, miraculous things will happen. Ideas will flow. Problems will be solved. Hurt will be healed. Solutions will show up. But you've got to DECIDE, COMMIT and TAKE ACTION. And a mastermind is a perfect lab for that to take place. The wins that come out of there can be turned into inspirational and actionable content for the rest of your tribe and customer base.

Now, let's make a quick language distinction here. I use the word "client" for anyone I am doing a service for, mentoring, or taking under my wing. I am committed to their results 100 percent as if my life and reputation depends on it, because it does. I use the word "customer" for anyone who purchases a product from me, whether it be digital or physical. Both of these people are your boss. But one you will have an intimate relationship with and one you simply will not. And that's a mutual thing. There is no desire when someone buys a product at a store or on Amazon for the creator of that product to reach out and be their buddy.

But when you take someone under your wing as a client, it's a completely opposite expectation. They want you to do whatever it takes to get it done. Boundaries are healthy, but great boundaries really come from setting client expectations properly from the get-go. If you provide a 24/7 service, that's the standard you must uphold. If there are specific times you meet on a regular basis, that's a different story. Whether you have a customer or a client, their communication channels and boundaries are clearly set by you in the beginning of that relationship. And if you or they feel like a boundary needs to be communicated better, it's a simple conversation to have.

You are the leader, however, so it's up to you to remain patient, clearly communicate and reestablish that boundary based on mutual communication. Take their expectations and yours and use them to meet in the middle and form agreements that you can both write down. Normally this takes the form of a contract, but it can be as simple as a quick recap via text or email after a discussion, listing the bullet points of what was discussed. If you've been in business for any appreciable length of time, you've probably had an experience or two with a nightmare client. It's ok to fire clients. One bad one can suck up the time, energy and attention you need to devote to 3-5 great ones.

But you should always seek to communicate and understand where they are coming from first. Sometimes you can set people up on a track to succeed with you just by creating better agreements. It is your responsibility as a leader to do so, even when you are not "at fault." In order to make the client relationship go smoothly and set proper agreements around outcomes, boundaries and communication, (the ABCs of great business relationships) the following questions should be asked in the onboarding call to establish a powerful frame with your client. It pays to get clear on the following things during the call:

# SUCCESS MAPPING CALL

*(With thanks and credit to Alex Moscow and Jennifer Hudye, reprinted with permission.)*

CLIENT NAME:

DATE:

ATTENDEES:

CALL RECORDING LINK:

## SET INTENTION FOR CALL

- How to win the game
- Roles of the team:
    - Reach out to Kyle for….
    - Reach out to Priya for…
    - Reach out to me for…

## WHAT WINNING LOOKS LIKE FOR YOU

1. What is the #1 problem you came to us to solve, or want to have in progress towards solving?
2. What additional outcomes would make our time together a total WIN?
3. WHY are you committed to succeeding in life, and in this program RIGHT NOW? (What will results do for you/your family/future/etc.?)
4. What is your go-to when you hit resistance?
5. So, how might you fuck this up? (What are your sabotage patterns? —freak out, withdraw, etc.)
6. What specific actions can you set up to prevent that?

7. How can we/the community support you in following through on those actions?
8. Regarding feedback, how honest and direct would you want it on a scale of 1-10?
9. What is an example of a level ____ feedback that was given to you and it was well received?

## VALUE

10. What is your favorite client result?
11. What does your pricing look like?
12. How will you reward yourself for completion of this program/your commitments/etc.?

## COMMUNICATION

We are not here to be liked and to tell you what you want to hear. We are here to support you and call you forward to a higher level of greatness and tell you what you need to hear.

## WHAT WINNING LOOKS LIKE FOR US

- I as the client agree to:
    o Show up on the calls,
    o Ask questions when I need support,
    o Check in with the kind of support that I need.
- One (1) module completed each week (if there is a course component to the mastermind)
    o Time to complete logged in calendar weekly
- Show up to group calls and private calls
- Contribute to Facebook group, ask questions, share wins, offer insights
- Reach out if struggling or feeling deep resistance can't work through on own
- Group call and Facebook posting best practices

- IF your desires on HOW to win changes or what solutions you desire, come to us to recalibrate and support you in the new direction

## WHAT ARE YOUR IMMEDIATE NEXT STEPS

- What are you specifically committed to completing this week?
- What's your deadline for that?
- How will you reward yourself for that win?

What I've noticed after many years of doing this now is that people get addicted to masterminding, they see how effective it is and they see how with each session their last, biggest challenge became no big deal anymore. I have yet to encounter a problem that can persist in the light of this group work. And they're ready and excited to work on whatever shows up next as a challenge or something they want to simply move faster on. They go from being stuck and feeling out of sorts or even worse, *worthless*, to feeling alive again because they're stoked at how much progress they're making. It's truly a gift to watch and I want others to take this model and repeat it in their local communities as a service. You'll be amazed at how many people will come to you with open arms, sometimes in tears wanting you to be more involved in their lives, eager to help you however and with whatever they can, and how deep the relationships can get on all fronts.

And if you want to do this professionally for money, the best way to get the reps in is to do it for your local community on a weekly basis. We do ours every Wednesday night from 6:00 p.m. to 9:00 p.m., with the last hour being for networking. It's really become an incredible group. The Facebook group recently crossed 400 members and we routinely have 15-20 people show up per week! We've had to limit the hot seats to 10 but we usually can get everyone in if we keep it tight, and the group gets stronger as time goes on as well.

If you're interested in doing this as a paid part of your business, it's an amazing model.

The best part is you get to make this your own. You'll quickly get the hang of it and create such a powerful community of conscious co-creators. It's crazy! Provided it's valuable, it will grow unbelievably quickly. And the relationships you'll form as a result will stand the test of time.

To help you scale, you'll want to gather bit by bit incredible testimonials. The best of these are the most *emotional*.

# EMOTIONAL TESTIMONIAL GUIDELINES
## WITH CREDIT TO MARTIN LATULIPPE

Here are a few emotional testimonial guidelines and elicitation questions to help (Inspired by Martin Latulippe). Some key points of a great testimonial include:

- When I met Brad, I was doing, living etc.
- I had this concrete problem
- This is how Brad helped
- The results I've had in my life
- The results I've had in my business
- The domino effects to other areas of my life
- The ripple effects to other people in my life.
- The cost of not working with Brad would be
- The resultant urge to take action

Emotion in these testimonials is not only welcome but encouraged! Urge them to share more, especially if it's moving.

## QUESTIONS

- "What was your life and business like before you met Brad?"
- "What was a specific, concrete problem you were facing in your life or business?"
- "How did Brad help you, specifically?"
- "What are the results you've had in your life since working with Brad?"
- "What about your business? What results have you had there?"
- "What are some other areas of your life that have been affected as a result?"
- "How have others in your life benefitted from the transformations you've made in your life and business?"
- "Tell us more about that."
- "What would be the cost of not working with Brad?"
- "What would you say to someone who is considering working with Brad to improve their life or business?"
- "Anything else you want the people at home to know?"
- "Thank you so much for sharing your story, we are grateful as it will help us help others like you."

# 5 SIMPLE STEPS

Building successful masterminds is nearly impossible, of course, if you don't have a *plan*. In fact, let's get right into the basics of your own plan right now. The following pages will give you all the steps at a high level, leaving many of the specifics for your own mastermind(s) for you to create. To get you going, we have proven step-by-step scripts, endless hours of training, and many other resources to help you nail this, but there are limits to what I can provide in one book.

Nonetheless, without further ado, let's look at *How to Build a Mastermind in 5 Simple Steps*:

1. Dream It
2. Research It
3. Test It
4. Nail It
5. Scale It

## Step One: Dream It

Take some time to consider and journal as much as you can on the following questions, tightening and clarifying as you go:

- What is most important to you in having a mastermind?
- What do you want to earn?
- Who do you want to work with?
- How many people do you want to impact? In what ways?
- Mindset and Values: WHY do you want success?

What will it look like, feel like, and how will you know when you get there? Get hyper clear on your vision, or work with us to help you!

## STEP TWO: RESEARCH IT

You must have *conversations* with people whom you want to help and ask them about their problems, how long they've been having the problem, what they've tried to fix it in the past or are currently doing to compensate for it, what the cost of not solving it is, and what their dream solution would look like.

How does the problem make them feel emotionally? What are their angers, anxieties, frustrations, as well as their goals, dreams, and desires?

This will not only help you gain clarity on your offer, but will help tap into the emotional drivers behind their decisions and craft copy, messaging, and videos that speak directly to that, so when you implement Step 5 (not yet!) you'll be ready.

You'll also need to ask skilled questions in order to understand their most persistent and pressing problem, how they currently go about solving it, what happens if they don't, and what, if anything, they'd be willing to pay to solve it.

Then you can create your offer, which you then *test* by *selling* it before you *build it*.

## STEP THREE: TEST IT

Come up with an MVP or MPE (minimum viable product or experience). As I said, you need to take what you learned in the previous step and formulate it into a hypothetical mastermind offer that you can test through selling it to 10-50 people. If it's something like a mastermind or coaching, 5-10 test clients who actually buy your first one is plenty.

People must pay money for this (not as much as they will when it's complete, and give them a money back guarantee if they're not satisfied with the product or service).

Be willing to have 25-50 sales conversations to get the feedback you need to decide whether this is a good idea to pursue or not.

Ideally, you do a one-off mastermind (½ day to 2 days) to prove out the concept which you can then expand into a 3, 6, or 12-month offer.

If they won't buy under these pilot/beta circumstances, they won't buy *ever*. Remember that. That's a big red flag and means the mastermind you were intending to build probably doesn't have the demand you need for it to be sustainable.

Remember, the most successful entrepreneurs always report the phenomenon of their business taking off after multiple failed attempts because they found a gold vein of an offer and made it.

The right market fit is EVERYTHING. It's *so* worth it to wait until you find it. And it's totally okay jettisoning the idea, tweaking or abandoning it for the next best idea. Don't be afraid to keep asking questions and trying things until you get something with traction.

## Step Four: Nail It

Once you've tested it by selling it, now it's time to refine and perfect it. You do this by working with your beta clients, getting feedback through surveys, tweaking and iterating, answering their questions through content and expert interviews, and getting it just right.

Once you've got it, it's really easy to do the next part, which is to get amazing testimonials, social proof (screenshots are best), and case studies from your first batch of clients/customers.

Take a look at some of our collected testimonials here so you get the idea: http://buildamastermind.com/testimonials.

These bits are GOLD when you go to create additional assets like sales pages, copy, and webinars in order to market and sell your mastermind at scale, because you now have everything you need for step FIVE.

## STEP 5: SCALE IT

Once you have your offer nailed, you are ready to scale! Now the fun part comes. You don't have to do this all at once, but you'll want to start creating lead magnets to attract leads, and eventually lower-priced offers so you can run ads profitably and scale.

You'll take all the market research data you've compiled from the previous steps and use it to attract your ideal customers and clients in a world of noise.

When you get this right, it's very powerful!

One of my clients makes $9 for every $1 he spends on Instagram ads in his niche (a mastermind for cops).

If you built a machine where you put a dollar in and nine came out, how many dollars would you put in the machine?

As many as possible, of course!

While the ins and outs of paid traffic and funnels aren't in the purview of this book, and you can absolutely scale to $100k/year without them, paid acquisition are the *only* way to reliably scale a business. Organic is great, referrals are great, but the path to scale is through *paid traffic*.

So whether you're just starting or have been at this for years, we have many options to help you scale when you're ready. But if you need help, you need to raise your hand and take action. If it's a good fit, we'll work together to get this off the ground.

I've done everything I can within the context of a book. Now it's time to decide: Are you going to *build a mastermind* of your own?

We're here for you. Apply now to see if you qualify:

http://buildamastermind.com/schedule-now

## WANT EVEN MORE?

Have a listen to me walking my client Chavaun through this overview of how to go from zero to scaling your mastermind here: http://marbles.link/MMLaunchOverview.

# ADDITIONAL MASTERMIND MARKETING AND SALES RESOURCES

So now that we've learned how to run a mastermind, be it in person or virtually, we need to actually *sell* one. We have multiple tools to help you do this. Some are paid, some are free. I would love to be able to include all of these in print, but some require more of an audio/visual experience to deliver, and some are more advanced trainings we offer, which are paid:

1. First, you have this book in your hand (or on your device)

2. You have the audio version here: http://8minutemastermind.com/audio

3. You have the full 21-day *Build A Mastermind Platinum Challenge* here: http://buildamastermindchallenge.com

4. You have the *Offers Creation Domination Mini-Course* here: http://buildamastermind.com/offer

5.  You have the *Sales Masterclass* here:
    http://buildamastermind.com/sales

6.  Here's our training on the *Five Shifts* that will allow
    you to build a $100k+ mastermind:
    http://mastermindfaster.com (free for 48 hours after
    signing up)

7.  You have the community of thousands of bad-asses
    here:
    http://facebook.com/groups/mastermindsforentrepren
    eurs

8.  And if you are the type who doesn't want to waste
    time figuring this all out on your own, and you need
    or want help from our team with implementing all of
    this and having us coach you each step of the way,
    you can apply for our program which will help you do
    that here: http://buildamastermind.com/schedule-
    now

9.  You can find some great testimonials here:
    http://buildamastermind.com/testimonials

# CONCLUSION

"What if we could tune out, stop being afraid and over consuming all the time? What if we could begin anew with a renewed sense of beauty and grace and connectedness to the world at large? What if we were no longer afraid to trust our fellow humans, but just loved them by default? I'm here to say, it's not only possible, it's a much better strategy."

—BRAD HART

# BE LIMITLESS

WHEN I STARTED, I was lost, disillusioned and alone. In 2010, I had just lost my dad. Family squabbles and infighting over money soon led to losing relationships with a significant number of family members as well. People are always telling you who they really are, if you care to listen. I took that pain and I knew I had to make it mean something positive. I've always felt at an innate level that I had something unique that would give all the pain I've experienced a purpose. But what I really wanted was to feel like I belonged... And I had no idea how to belong with the people I wanted to belong with.

Maybe you can relate?

Leadership starts with self-leadership, so I made it a point to get into shape, develop new skills and fail (read: learn) a lot. I didn't know the way, but I was committed. I tried everything and over the next several years invested over $500,000 into self-development, masterminds, travel, trips, coaching, mentorship, lessons and more. It wasn't easy, and I was going it alone, with no network and no support.

Nobody believed in me at first. Sometimes, even I didn't believe in myself. But I was committed to learning what I didn't' know, so I read a lot of books and did my best to surround myself with world class individuals. I got in front of people like Richard Branson, Tim Ferriss, Neil Strauss and others whose work had inspired or impacted me in some way up until that point. I wasn't yet at a level (or at least that was my story at the time) where I could add significant value to any of these relationships. Even if they did provide me with the opportunity to do so (they did) I wasn't able and willing to capitalize on it.

My mindset wasn't there.

Since then, it's shifted drastically and irrevocably, forever. It took me 8-9 months to really get my local free mastermind dialed in, but it's conferred so many benefits to the community and me I can no longer picture my life without it now. I've had so many opportunities open up and amazing things happen as a result of leading this mastermind that I can't really believe it. I'm so grateful for it every single day, and the people who attend often really get to be like a family. It's so gratifying to see people come week after week and keep crushing their challenges, evolving, and growing. All in just 8-10 minutes of dedicated time per person, per week! I don't know of a single other method that allows so many people to have such massive breakthroughs in such a short period of time.

If you've been following my posts on Facebook, you'll see the work we're doing around the world, the experiences, the world-class people, the magic moments, and the impact we're making.

Meanwhile multiple projects are in motion back home with little or no input from me. For examples:

- Make More Marbles has a new partner website for our work with masterminds at

  www.buildamastermind.com

  We've created a video with the Draw Shop (one of those white boards with the voice over) to illustrate the message and the brand.

- We're booking world-class podcast guests left and right. Real game changers in their industries with epic wisdom to share. Our content game is strong—over 50k people have reacted to our posts in some way (FB just started sharing these things from my personal profile) and that's just organic on my profile. The connections are easily in the millions and 15k people read our stuff daily now.

- We've sold out and OVER-booked multiple trips and retreats this year, each with 50+ entrepreneurs and game changers, doing everything from refugee work, to headed to China, Tony Robbins, and more.

- We have TWO books now, the one you now hold and another titled, _The Choice_, which was a collaborative project with the Abundant Purpose Mastermind. It's magic. I'm a proud papa penguin.

We're making ACTUAL marbles to strengthen our ability to enroll, influence, and impact people with our brand and message around the world. More coming on this front, but it's going to be SO FREAKING SWEET. We're planning more trips, creating more masterminds, and growing the ability to serve at ever higher levels every day. And the sales keep coming whether I'm here or there or anywhere. I've done more traveling this month than I used to make in a year, and I'm reinvesting a MASSIVE portion of it into new projects, infrastructure, and investments.

The leadership qualities you gain from masterminds are mind boggling. Knowing that at any time you can command the attention of 20 people and get them to work together without being the "guy in charge" but simply a facilitator for the process gives you a sense of confidence across all areas of life that is next to none. I've hosted webinars with 3,000 people, spoken on stages large and small, given countless presentations and done more live online events than I can count. I credit masterminds with giving me the sense of community, leadership confidence, belonging, worthiness, and purpose that we all crave in life.

My goal is that at least 1,000 other people start mastermind groups of their own and stick with it for at least one year. If the average size grows to even 10, that's 10,000 people who will be deeply transformed by this work. I want YOU starting your own mastermind(s), and I've made it as easy as I can with my Build a Mastermind (BAM) program (see the back of the book) and my FREE BUILD A MASTERMIND 21-Day Challenge, which you can access here:

www.buildamastermind.com/challenge

Another initiative is to start a mastermind with 6-10 billionaires who are committed to global systemic change around our F.U.S.E. goals: Food, Utilities, Shelter and Education.

The Make More Marbles Mindset encompasses not only abundance—we want to *be more, do more, give more*—but also to realize that you already have everything you've ever needed to live your true purpose and impact massive amounts of people in a positive way, creating untold wealth in the process. And wealth is not just money. It's world-class health, relationships, experiences and more.

We all win more through collaboration, and team work makes the dream work. When you have the right person to call at the right time, it's like playing the game of business with cheat codes. I lost $45,000 on my first business venture because I simply didn't know what I didn't know. Since then, we've had million-dollar months. I see many people going down the same path toward inevitable failure, and while we can't save them all, I can save the ones that are swimming towards us.

What's more, the message resonates with people. They look at the world in a different way and create more incredible magic than they ever thought possible. It's not because the world has changed. It's because *they* have changed. A true leader doesn't create more followers, they create more *leaders*. So I'm here today telling you all of this because I have a leadership opportunity for those who are ready to step up, put their ego aside, and truly come from a place of service and gratitude. The funny thing about growth and contribution is more comes back to you than you could have ever possibly imagined. Life is like a big mirror—you're always getting back exactly what you're putting out. If you focus on being more, doing more and giving more, having more is the natural result. If you focus just on what you're going to get . . . not so much.

You must render service at the level in which you want to receive, which requires growth. You must be willing to invest in yourself if others are to invest in you. This is not for everyone and there will be work to do, but nothing that's worth it is also easy. Life wants to give you exactly what you want, and it does that by giving you the challenges that grow you and shape you into the person you need to become for those things to show up effortlessly for. You can have anything you need, want, and desire provided you are willing to help others get what they need, want, and desire. The secret to living is GIVING. I've seen it in my own life in a multitude of ways, and so have the thousands our work has impacted.

I get messages almost every day from people who are quitting their jobs, starting businesses, getting into shape, ditching alcohol, finding their purpose and alignment, growing their teams, making more money, learning all the systems and skills to not only pay the bills but to finally thrive on their own terms. And the best part is the domino and ripple effects go on forever. Your legend lives on, even when you're gone. We make more marbles, but we also make more marble makers and marble-making machines.

And it's all because I was willing to go first, give first, and trust. I didn't know the way forward, but I was committed, so I found the way. That's what we intend to help you do as well with the Build a Mastermind program that we're kicking off. There's never a hard sell here, but I'll ask you a question:

Do you believe that things happen for a reason?

If you've read this far, don't you think this is something to which you were meant to give serious consideration?

I want you to find your flow and create the teams you need to build the dreams you have. So I want you to share this message if it resonated with you. I would love if it reached the people who truly need it, so feel free to tag someone who's a great fit. Why, you ask?

This is a key point, so read carefully:

*You must be willing to give away to others what you wish to receive yourself. What you think the world is withholding from you, you may just be withholding from the world.*

You will win, and you will learn, but as long as you never give up, you will make this a part of your life for the long term, helping a lot of people, making a lot of money (both directly if you choose to start a paid mastermind and indirectly through connections and opportunities) and most importantly of all, having a lot of FUN!

When you marry that with a give-first mentality, there is no limit to the heights you can achieve.

# BUILD A

# MASTERMIND!

**I help people start and grow profitable, thriving mastermind communities.**

Join my FREE *BUILD A MASTERMIND CHALLENGE* today!
Click the link below to learn more.

**ﱡﱡﱡﱡ BUILD A MASTERMIND**

https://buildamastermind.com/challenge

# GET PAID!

When you're ready to transition some of your free mastermind members to PAID masterminds, we have a bunch of additional trainings on transitioning from free to paid, including our flagship Build A Mastermind Program.

And when you're interested in taking your *paid* MM to the next level, I'm certain I can add some great strategies to your tool belt.

Book a call if you want to discuss. Here's a link to my calendar:

buildamastermind.com/schedule-now

# GIVE A FREE PHYSICAL COPY OF THIS BESTSELLING BOOK!

JUST PAY SHIPPING!

https://buildamastermind.com/book

# ABOUT THE AUTHOR

### BRAD HART

Founder of Make More Marbles

WITH 20 YEARS as an entrepreneur and 16 years managing wealth under his belt, Brad Hart is committed to helping entrepreneurs and investors reach their full potential, so they can focus on solving the grand challenges of our time.

With extensive experience in real estate, investments, trading, marketing, sales, and peak performance strategy, he's built and helped build several companies, growing revenues and profits into the millions of dollars. His hedge fund, Hartwood Capital, returned 106% in profit in a single year.

From co-leading a mastermind of 52 people in China and Hong Kong, to holding mastermind groups in Bali, Italy, Greece, and all over the U.S., Brad has been a part of 28 masterminds and started 10 himself, including a local weekly mastermind group with 400 members.

Brad is founding member of the Knowledge Business Blueprint (KBB) speaking/training team led by Tony Robbins and Dean Graziosi, a community and self-education movement which has helped tens of thousands of people to launch their own masterminds.

**Build A Mastermind** (or BAM for short) is his latest initiative, helping entrepreneurs to add $100k+ to their businesses in profit per year with only 5-10 hours a month ongoing time commitment.

Brad is a graduate of Binghamton University where he received a BS in biology and rowed on the crew team, as well as worked as an EMT.

Brad grew up in New York and now lives in San Diego, California.

# BONUS CHAPTER

## HOW TO RUN A VIRTUAL MASTERMIND, STEP-BY-STEP

AS YOU NO DOUBT KNOW, the whole world is now practicing physical distancing to keep themselves and others safe from Covid-19. I think that's definitely the right move, given the dangers this virus poses. But that does NOT mean that we have to practice SOCIAL distancing, as the news might encourage you to do.

Why? Simple.

The words we choose define (and therefore create) our realities. I see the effects of "social distancing" everywhere I go. People are shy to even say hello and won't even make eye contact—It's kinda sad. They've been told they need to be SOCIALLY distancing (poor choice of words) and they've taken that to mean there should be NO interaction whatsoever. And we need to change that.

People are hurting more than ever, and if this continues, it will only get worse. Therefore, they need your leadership and love now more than ever. What better way to get your social interaction on during quarantine than with a mastermind? It's like a peer support group where you actually take action and get your challenges solved. And it's easier now than ever to start one!

I'll give you three options to start a virtual mastermind—for beginners, intermediate, and advanced folks:

## BEGINNER

**Step One:** Get Zoom (http://zoom.us). Log in and get familiar with the platform and how it works by going to http://zoom.us/test. Make sure you understand at least the basics, and grab the link to your zoom room.

**Step Two:** Pick a date and time you will host your mastermind.

**Step Three:** Announce date and time on social media, inviting people to join at the link.

**Step Four:** Mastermind with the people who show up! How? Simply spotlight each person for a hot seat, including yourself!

Here's the format for each hot seat:

- Who are you and what do you do? (30 seconds)
- What are you grateful for/celebrating? (30 seconds)
- What is your challenge or something you want to move faster on? (60 seconds)
- Have the entire group ask clarifying questions, make suggestions. (3-5 mins)
- Encourage them to make a declaration on their next action steps, timing this. (60 Seconds)

This should take about eight (8) minutes when you get really good at it :)

That's it! Record the call so they have it handy if they need to refer back (Sometimes hot seats can be a little overwhelming and people forget to take notes, but boy do they work!).

Here are 50+ recordings of hotseats so you can hear how it works: http://marbles.link/hotseats

## INTERMEDIATE

Do everything in *Beginner*, but add a simple funnel, with a Google Spreadsheet, Zapier (see www.zapier.com to learn more), and a ClickFunnels page like ours:

http://mrbls.co/clickfunnels

Grab a custom domain if you like. Make it pretty (Don't just copy ours verbatim, please use your own assets and creativity.) and send that link to folks through a two-step post on social media or a traditional email if you have a list.

Then, when they sign up you'll have their emails, names, challenges, and the order they submitted on the sheet.

Sample copy for FB: "Who wants to join my FREE virtual mastermind this week?"

When you go live, share your screen so the spreadsheet is visible to everyone, so they know their place in the queue, and you don't waste time going through all the preamble. You can just call on people and rock out—We had over 40 people join ours last week with almost zero notice off one social media post, so people will definitely join yours.

If you need help beyond this, we have DIY resources for you in the book funnel:

**Our book funnel (free, just pay shipping)**

http://8minutemastermind.com/free

And you can buy them and absorb them to your heart's content. They will get you well on your way.

## ADVANCED

Do everything in *Beginner* and *Intermediate*, but now add a backend offer:

10. Use an online scheduler like **Calendly** or create a form on Google Docs to connect or book calls (See example here: buildamastermind.com/schedule-now).
11. Hook up **Calendly** with **Zoom** so it sends a link out to the person who books automatically.
12. Once you have that and your offer set up (see http://buildamastermind.com/offer for training on offers), just mention it on the call and in follow-up communication that you are helping _____ to _____ through _____ (your value statement) and add "would that be of value to you or not?"
    (The three blanks above are (1) ideal client, (2) outcome you help them achieve, and (3) vehicle. For example: "I help entrepreneurs to add $100k+ to their businesses in 5-10 hours a month with virtual masterminds."

If they're a YES, simply send your calendar invite, and you're done!

Now, I know this isn't the full picture. There's a LOT to building a profitable business online. Here's a partial list of things you'll have to master in order to make it work.

- Picking your niche
- Copywriting
- Marketing
- Sales
- Follow up
- Messenger outreach
- Email list management

- Creating content
- 2-step posts
- Hiring
- Systems
- Delegation
- Facebook groups
- Building a profitable lead generation funnel
- Running ads
- Charging top dollar for your coaching, consulting packages, and masterminds
- Delivering and over-delivering on value, creating raving fans in the process.

All of this without going broke or wanting to pull your hair out. It can be the challenge of a lifetime to figure this out on your own, so that's why we have the Build A Mastermind Program. Listen, if you're cool with free advice and want to implement on your own, you certainly can, but make no mistake, it will take a lot longer and probably cost you a lot more money and wasted time which you can never get back. OR you can learn directly from me, my team of experts, and my clients who are already doing it.

Let's be real for a moment. If free advice worked, then in the age of YouTube and Google, everyone would be a shredded billionaire, in their dream relationship, about to achieve enlightenment. But we're not. And that's because people pay attention to *what they pay for* and *what pays them.*

And in this increasingly complex world, you must be willing to invest in mentorship and get the right knowledge to implement the right things at the right time, or you'll get little-to-no results.

So if you're ready to make a real investment in yourself and your business to get to the next level, apply for a spot in our program (limited availability):

www.Buildamastermind.Com/schedule-now

I look forward to welcoming you into the BAM FAM with us and seeing you crush it! Let's help a lot of people, have a lot of fun, and make a lot of money together!

Limited spots left—are you my next dream client?

Sending love from sunny California,

~ B

P.S. Want proof? Here's a bunch of screenshots I grabbed of real people just like you crushing it with us right now in the program:

http://bit.ly/MMproof

# APPENDICES

"If you want to be a billionaire, help a billion people."
—PETER DIAMANDIS

# APPENDIX A:

# MASTERMIND

# EXAMPLES

TO SEE A MASTERMIND in action, I recently did a small one for a few of my clients in time zones on the opposite side of the world. Watch the video now to get a real sense of what a mastermind is like and how they run (breakthroughs galore!).

http://mrbls.co/MastermindExample

*(Case sensitive—the M and the E must be capitalized*

*for the link to work.)*

For more audio you can also check out our mastermind podcast which will be live soon here:

https://makemoremarbles.com/podcasts/

# APPENDIX B:

# SOCIAL MEDIA POST

## SAMPLE SOCIAL MEDIA POST TO PROMOTE YOUR MASTERMIND

ON THE FOLLOWING PAGES is an iteration of posts I've used in the past to fill my mastermind. Some have gotten 100+ comments and dozens of shares! Feel free to use a similar flow and format for yours:

# LIMITED OPPORTUNITY—BE MENTORED BY ME AND MY TEAM

AS ALWAYS, members of my team and I have been reaching out to you in an effort to see what you're struggling with most, and how we can best serve your needs. Like a paddling of Long Island Mallards, we may seem calm and collected on the surface of the water, but our little legs are kicking hard underneath. I get a minimum of dozens, sometimes hundreds of notes, emails, PM's and texts from entrepreneurs each day from all over the world, and I know I speak for the whole MMM (Make More Marbles) team when I say we're grateful to be of service. First of all, I want to acknowledge and thank the dozens of people who have responded to our requests, hopped on the phone with us, and shared their aspirations.

I've been writing a lot lately about my journey in entrepreneurship, mentoring others, building masterminds, investing, Amazon, crypto/blockchain, going to Hong Kong, China, Greece, Italy, Tony Robbins UPW (Unleash the Power Within), Mexico (still spots left!), giving back in Syrian refugee camps, shelters and schools, and exploring new opportunities. I want to contribute to this community on a higher level, and I have a way to do that, but we'll get to that in a minute. As promised, I'm pleased to announce the results of this 'Ask' style campaign and what has come out of it. If you also serve and support entrepreneurs like us, you'll find the following quite valuable.

First, the things that entrepreneurs are asking for most:

- "How do I generate more leads?"
- "How do I stay accountable?"
- "How do I find mentors?"
- "What mastermind should I join?"
- "How do I make more sales?"

- "I hate doing certain things in my business, but I can't afford to hire someone yet. What do I do?"
- "How can I learn how to tell my story better and attract the clients I want?"
- "How can I serve more people and make more money?"
- "How can I be more productive so that I can spend more time with my family and on things that truly matter?"
- "How do I find a tribe or a group to both contribute to and be supported by?"
- "I'm tired of the noise, the scams, the promises that I'm going to 'get rich quick', I know it's all nonsense, but what IS legit?"
- "How do I invest the money I'm making to work for me, instead of me working for money? I'm tired of the grind. (HUGE)"
- "How do I diversify both my income streams AND my investments to balance risk and decrease uncertainty about the future?"
- "I love what I'm doing and it pays the bills, but I want so much more now. How do I find a better vehicle to create the life I envision and serve the people I want to serve?"

Our mission has always been to help entrepreneurs increase their impact, influence, income, investments and infrastructure so they can be more, do more, and give more. All of these questions are a function of three ways we serve and support entrepreneurs at Make More Marbles:

- Messaging
- Masterminding
- Mentorship

Yes, we love alliteration. Also, black and white animals. Let's quickly break down each one.

*Messaging* is how you tell your story, educate your audience, add value, and create a relationship where they don't just know you, but also like you and trust you. You become the trusted expert in their eyes. By doing so, you generate qualified, interested leads who will love to hear about your product or service. It's also how you turn those interested and qualified leads into paying customers and clients and make sales. Since all businesses exist to serve people, without people who pay you money in exchange for value of some sort, you don't have a business. What if you could generate leads and sales on demand in a variety of ways? How would that help you grow your business at will?

*Masterminding* is how you get the support and insights you need to both move faster with less stagnant energy and create less friction as you execute on ideas in your business. It gives you an incredible edge on those who are trying to go at it alone, or just assuming the answers will show up in a book or some clickbait listicle on the internet somewhere. What if you had the combined brainpower, connections and resources of other successful entrepreneurs at your fingertips? What if you knew the answer was just a quick text or phone call away?

*Mentorship* is the last key piece of the puzzle. The right mentors in life are the difference between success and failure. They can be a steady guiding hand throughout your journey. I say the "right" ones because not just any will do. You need mentors with similar strengths, skill sets, and most importantly those who have the things in their lives that you WANT, because otherwise they'll give you a lot of great advice that doesn't work for you. It's the same reason why Warren Buffett, mentored by Benjamin Graham, teamed up with Charlie Munger, were able to create more wealth than anyone on the planet. They're people who understand numbers and timing and were a perfect fit for one another. What if you had the PERFECT mentor to guide you along the path toward creating wealth and living your purpose? How would that shift things for you and your business? How far could you go? How fast?

That brings me to the next point. Who's on your team? And how are you spending your TEAM resources? Who is your TEAM playing for? Teamwork makes the dream work. Nothing of merit is ever accomplished alone. We love to hear the stories of Elon Musk, Richard Branson, Steve Jobs, and Bill Gates. They're inspiring, but their success isn't due to them working in a room alone somewhere. They may have gotten the ball rolling, but their companies are comprised of hundreds of thousands of people who work in harmony with one another toward the realization of their big vision. Just like them, no matter how talented you are and no matter how hard you're willing to work, you still only have a finite amount of Time, Energy, Attention, and Money.

Now, Energy and Attention you can increase by a) not wasting It or b) through increasing your capacity through various methods, which increases the quality of your time. Even then, time is limited. Only 24 hours a day, 168 hours a week. Whether you're a master of the universe like Tony Robbins or Warren Buffett or the guy on the street hawking watches, you still have the same amount of time.

So where do you get more leverage? First, you need to become more productive and use your time in the best way possible. Forming the right habits is paramount. As you become more masterful with this skill, even rest, fun, and recovery become both intentional and more important than ever, because they become the fuel that allows you to get the most out of your productive time.

Second, you must be able to control your emotions, that's how you feel at any given time. This is the difference between failing and succeeding, and whether you feel good along the way.

Finally, it's the people you surround yourself with that make the difference. If you don't have the right support, accountability and community behind you, you will never make it past the first roadblock you encounter. You see, balance is key in all things. This allows you to be more productive, live in your strengths, and find your flow on demand. The more productive time you have and the more you live in YOUR flow and YOUR strengths, the more money you will be able to earn, and the bigger and better team you will be able to build. Then your team's Time, Energy and Attention is also working on your vision, and you get to grow as a leader and contribute at a higher level than you ever thought possible.

All businesses need two sets of four things:

1. **First set**: Ideas, People, Timing, and Numbers.
2. **Second set**: Leads, Sales, Value delivery, and Operations.

We can mentor you the correct way to get the results you want, need and desire, build a team to suit your strengths, and drastically shorten your learning curve as an entrepreneur, which is good for you, the people you serve, and the world.

If you're already successful, great! We will pour gasoline on your fire by supporting you in the expansion of your vision and mission, growing your business to new heights, and creating a legacy of giving and contribution. We will help make the connections you need to get to the next level. We all want to get from where we are to where we want to go. Or close the gap. But the vehicle you choose (your business model) is just as important as the driver (you!).

So why me? I'll share more in a minute, but long story short, I'm equipped for the task. I've started and helped start dozens of million-dollar businesses, mentored many world-class entrepreneurs, and made, missed out on, and lost millions of dollars over the years. I've been to the top of the mountain and the bottom of the valley. There is not a problem that my team or my network of mentors and connections can't solve. This is not hyperbole. I'm like an entrepreneurial owl. Always asking 'who, who, who', as is my strength, I've built your dream network over the last decade. My team and I have helped thousands of others do great things, make a lot of money, and live in passion and purpose. This is not meant to brag or impress you, but to impress UPON you what's possible.

Now, I don't do much private 1:1 coaching, which is why I prefer to run masterminds. I've started eight and been a member of 26 now. As much as I love both, I know I can make a bigger impact. However, I know my capacity to serve is limited by the vehicle I choose, which got me thinking, which then lead me to talking with all of you wonderful people. Conversations with front line entrepreneurs, to brand new entrepreneurs, to entrepreneurs making millions a month.

Messaging, Masterminding, Mentorship.

Without these three keys, massive success is unattainable. But we won't stop there. We'll also focus on the other intangible and tangible strategies, along with mindsets that make all the difference—productivity, teamwork, leadership, scaling, problem solving, and more.

What's more is the transition I'm making out of the services business and into the products business. I get countless requests from wonderful people who want a course or a class or to coach. I don't get lit up as much as I used to about each of these models, and honestly, they just don't scale to make the impact on the number of people that I truly want to make.

With all the smarmy crap and scams out there, I just don't see a lot of those vehicles aligning with my values going forward. So I've jettisoned a lot of projects to focus on three lanes. I call them my ABC's:

- Amazon
- Blockchain
- Contribution

These are where I'll be focusing my time from now on. Yes, I can help you build other types of businesses. But that's where I'll personally be focusing my energy. Each of these has a lot of subsections, but it helps me qualify opportunities immediately, and, just as importantly, say no to make room for the things I want to be a heck yes to, so I can live according to the laws of abundance and affluence:

*Make money, protect/grow money, give money away.*

And I'm still learning lessons each and every day. I know what it actually takes to be successful and have failed enough to know—sometimes you win, sometimes you learn. It's how you learn and grow and contribute more that allows you to be more, do more, give more, and yes: have more. But if having more money is the only reason you're getting into this, you're probably better off doing something else. I look at events the same way, we're doing them, and they're fun, but I know we're destined for more than just that. I see what many of my mentors put themselves through putting on these enormous productions just to make a bigger impact. Sometimes, they do. But it comes at a very real cost.

And like Tony Robbins—who doesn't need the money, like ever again—I'd rather do that from a place of complete contribution than feel I have to pay the bills. I know that I can help more people, but to live in integrity, I want the people I choose to help to actually succeed. The goal is to create 100 millionaires in the next 5 years. Not $1MM net worth. That's peanuts these days. You can't even buy a shoebox-sized apartment in Hong Kong for that anymore. $1MM a year or more in *income*. That's the new number. That's the level where real moving and shaking starts to happen.

But you'll never get there if you only focus on yourself and what you want. From Sara Blakely, the first self-made female billionaire and inventor of Spanx, I gleaned the following truth:

- If you focus on yourself, and your needs, wants and desires, you'll only make $75k-100k a year.
- If you focus on your family, maybe you'll increase that to $150-$250k/year.
- If you add in your tribe, your community, maybe $500k.
- But if you want to really make a huge impact, life supports you.

*Life supports that which supports life.*

You don't need a billion dollars. No one person could spend that money in 100 lifetimes, as it keeps replenishing itself if managed properly (which I can also teach you how to do, with strategies learned from the best in the world) and I will share what I've learned going down the rabbit hole in finance for years, even running my own successful hedge fund. But if your vision is large enough to encompass and impact enough people, billions are the natural result. As Peter

Diamandis says, "If you want to be a billionaire, help a billion people." The math checks out.

Look, I'm not trying to save anyone. That's not why I'm doing what I do. I've gotten over that. But if people are swimming toward me, and they want to make more marbles for everyone, I'm happy to help them. Like the Coast Guard, when the boat capsizes, they save the ones who are swimming towards them first, lest they may drown themselves. If you know me personally, you probably know that I lost my dad and my best friend in college to drinking. My dad, for sure, didn't want to be saved. Everyone has free will and a choice, and it takes two to tango. So, even though I desperately wanted to,... I couldn't save them. Now, I have a saying: "I don't light fires in people, I just throw gasoline on them." For the RIGHT people who just need to be plugged into the right opportunity at the right time, a mentor like me, access to resources, my network and mentors, and a team of mentors like mine can make all the difference. Got a big vision? I'm your guy. What's more is they'll have each other and the communal brain power, resources connections, experience and knowledge of one another.

This will not be for everyone. It can't be. I know I only have capacity to work with 10 people right now. Seven of those spots are already filled. So for these last three spots, there will be an investment and there will be an application. This will be slightly higher priced than my other masterminds and trips for obvious reasons, but cheaper and more accessible to more people than private coaching with me.

But you'll also get much, much more than I've ever offered before, as well as the support of my team and my network—accountability, support, masterminding, calls, 10 hours a month with my team, all our resources and trainings and ALSO one-on-one time with me.

And that's just the beginning. You'll get to see me build my own multiple multi-million-dollar businesses from the ground floor. They're not the first ones I've built, but they will be by far the biggest yet. That's right, I'm opening the kimono. You can ask me anything and if there are no conflicts or partners who don't want it shared, I'll share it. Complete transparency. Nothing to prove, nothing to hide, nothing to lose. My strategy. My wins. My losses. My investments. My team. My structure. My workflows. My processes. My systems. All of it. You'll have access to it all and can R&D (read: "Rob and Duplicate") whatever you want. Need something? Just ask your assigned mentor who fits your strength and wealth dynamics profile. You get 10 hours a month with my team, included.

Like Ben and Warren, you will go far together. And I'll be there to make certain you get what you need, when you need it. I'll be there to support too.

But I can't do this for everyone.

Let's talk about the cost.

I'm looking to make the cost irrelevant because for the right *three* (3) people (yes, that's as many as we're accepting into this program right now) this is worth at least 10 times what we will charge and potentially many millions in your future. I want this to be a massive win and change the lives of these three people. I will refund anyone and kick them out if they're not getting the value. I won't waste your time or mine. Just ask my team, I already have kicked people out. I'm here to win and help you win more. To make more marbles for everyone. I've made and lost and missed out on millions over the years. I've studied 1,000+ business models. I've had 6 100M+ mentors, including two well-known billionaires. I've spent over $600k on personal development, masterminds, coaching, and other investments in myself and my skill set.

What's more, is I've helped countless others double their revenue, increase their sales, balance their investments and risk, build teams, create billion-dollar campaigns and brands, live in abundance and purpose, and live and breathe their mission. I've also failed, a lot. Learned, loved and lost a lot too. I've been to the depths of hell and the depths of my soul. I've seen the top of the mountain and the bottom of the valley, and I'm ready to take you to the top in a way that not only aligns with your vision, it compels you to desire more than you ever thought possible. You won't achieve everything you've ever wanted, just to wonder "is that it?" either. Because you'll be living in flow, joy, and gratitude. You'll know you're living the life you were born to live.

Success without fulfillment is the ultimate failure, and I'll make sure you never experience anything but fulfillment along the way. Everything you want, everything you need, everything you desire. You will have it all and you will give more than you ever thought possible. The ripple effects of what you create, your legacy, will echo into eternity.

But it starts now, with this simple application. If you are unsure about the investment, or have questions, please reach out to me or the team. Or if you want to know what it's like to work with us, ask some of our clients!

Thanks for reading. This is limited to three (3) spots. If we open more spots in the future, they will be at a higher price. This has to keep being a good idea for everyone and in alignment with the laws of affluence and abundance. Don't wait. If this feels right, fill out the application and we'll be reaching out shortly.

Thanks gang! Suffice it to say I'm BEYOND excited for this. Three people are about to have their world rocked!

*Let's Make More Marbles!*

—B

P.S. In the spirit of abundance and in alignment with our values, we are also sponsoring one young entrepreneur. This spot is already filled, but if you're interested in being considered for a scholarship in the future, please share this post with your network and send us a PM saying why you would be a good fit.

# FOLLOW UP SUGGESTIONS

FOLLOW UP a day after with a single line post then you can reach out. Examples:

- **Mine:** "Who wants to build their own mastermind in 2019?"
- **Example for you:** "Who wants to join a mastermind this year?"

# APPENDIX C:

# TESTIMONIALS

ON THE PAGES that follow I'm sharing testimonials from people who have experienced some of the magic to be had from masterminds.

For more testimonials you can also visit:

www.buildamastermind.com/testimonials

## CHERILYN JONES

BEFORE I JOINED Brad's mastermind, I had been involved with other masterminds that were too large, unfocused, disorganized, and unsuccessful.

Brad's impact, contribution, coaching, and ability to put together a phenomenal mastermind is solid. He keeps them organized, focused, and offers high-level coaching. Therefore, they run successfully.

I've gained tremendous value and clarity through Brad's mastermind, and I've received tons of support from him and the rest of the group. He has provided a vehicle to allow me to contribute my skills and talents and receive from those of others. He is brilliant and clever with his knowledge of solving problems and providing solutions.

I highly recommend his expertise and especially his masterminds!"

—CHERILYN JONES

## SYLVIA BECKER-HILL

I'VE BEEN IN several masterminds, and in most of them, I felt like I had invested more than I had gained: time, money, love, my expertise, my connections. But that's not so with the masterminds that Brad designed and leads!

Brad's mastermind is brilliant for three reasons:

13. It attracts top-notch entrepreneurs who are willing to share their tricks of the trade and resources.
2.  It is simply structured and high-speed, not wasting a breath.
3.  I ALWAYS leave with a short list of implementable advice, action steps, and resources to connect with.

And this all happens in a sphere of love, integrity, and fun, which doesn't hurt either.

Thank you, Brad! You changed my life."

—SYLVIA BECKER-HILL

## STACEY SEGOWSKI

WHEN I JOINED Brad's mastermind, I was burnt out. My business felt like it was falling apart, and I didn't have the energy to fix it.

Going to his mastermind each week was my sanity saver. Not only did the mastermind help me cross off one big challenge each week in my business (and my life), but it helped me stay positive.

Several months later, I've found ways to have a bigger impact with my business while cutting my workload in half. I feel great, and I have more energy to spend time with loved ones and for traveling!

I've been a part of a lot of communities, and Brad's mastermind is seriously world-class. It's the perfect blend of focus, clarity, heart, and soul. "

—STACEY SEGOWSKI

## KYLIE McCONNELL

BRAD'S MASTERMIND has been one of the greatest investments for my business to date.

Before his mastermind, I was in multiple masterminds; however, I felt underwhelmed with the level of support—being too generic or watered down, which meant lackluster results.

Brad's structure is so clear, dependable, and concise that you have predictable, positive results consistently. The business, emotional, and strategic guidance I've received has resulted in better sales, clear messaging, and overall clarity and confidence in my business (from micro next steps to the macro WHY, which pulls me through).

Since I work with leaders and entrepreneurs to own their power and freedom, the clearer I am, the better THEIR results—so the ripple effect of masterminding with Brad continues to be enormous.

For anyone looking to upgrade their mastermind or start a mastermind, I highly recommend Brad Hart so that they get true, lasting results with the intimacy, accuracy, and powerful dynamic his masterminds provide. Our community appreciates Brad and what he provides so much!"

—KYLIE McCONNELL

## DANIEL EDWARD POWELL

BRAD IS AUTHENTIC. In a world where everything is delivered online or by an app, Brad gives what every human is craving: real, supportive human connection."

—DANIEL EDWARD POWELL

## TAMRA BOLTE

BEFORE BRAD'S MASTERMIND, I was feeling isolated as I tried to get answers to my questions myself and occasionally from well-meaning, but not so supportive family members.

It's a breath of fresh air to participate in a mastermind with others who've had success with things I'm trying to do. And it's extra nice to have a place where I contribute to others at the same time. It's nice to have a non-judgmental and positive-minded place to go for constructive input. Thanks, Brad."

—TAMRA BOLTE

## Samantha Hoffman

WHEN I MET Brad, I was working as an employee and was unsure of how to get to the next step in my life. I knew my end goal, but I didn't know what to do to get there. Through the mastermind group that Brad runs, he helped me obtain clarity on how to create the path to my end goal.

Brad builds a supportive and constructive space with his masterminds, allowing for collaboration with an incredibly varied group of people. I have seen in my own experiences, and in the experiences of those attending the mastermind on a regular basis, the profound impact of Brad's work.

The clarity, collaboration, and community I have gained since working with Brad are invaluable!

—Samantha Hoffman

## VANESSA PETERS

BRAD IS ABLE to bring together a group of people, many of them strangers, and create a safe space to reflect, receive feedback, and gain clarity on your life's issues.

I was amazed at how quickly he facilitates individuals coming together into a supportive group. The structure and pacing of the meeting gives the "hot seat" recipient valuable insights, and his quick presentations/feedback prevents overthinking by design.

Brad lives and breathes masterminds. Bringing people together for authentic connection is sorely missing in our society, and it's one of the basic human needs.

Thank you, Brad, for your important work."

—VANESSA PETERS

## Jannette Anderson

"JUST READ YOUR BOOK in one sitting and thought I would send you a testimonial for it.

Really LOVE the facilitator questions. Great resource which I really appreciate.

But after reading just the first three pages of the Preface, while I knew the content on Masterminds will be helpful, what I was inspired by was your ongoing example of authentic sharing. Not only does it call me to you, and to your realness, it calls me to my own. It illustrates and elicits my desire to be THAT kind of leader. Sharing. Loving. Real. Generous. Someone who gives permission to show up and shine in all of our shadow and light through example!

The book is about contributing through the power of masterminds and creating conscious communities of choice… but how you do what you do is the greatest teacher of all!

Thanks for the book—and the work that you do. You consistently inspire me to expand my context!

—Jannette Anderson
Founder of The Bodacity Project
Bodacity.ca

# DISCOVER THE PODCAST!

Want to hear ME run MY mastermind and get a ton of value from the hot seats while you're at it? Check out the *8-Minute Mastermind Podcast* (Don't forget to rate, subscribe, and share if you like it!).

https://makemoremarbles.com/podcasts/

Made in USA - Kendallville, IN
1135767_9781653306879
01.08.2021 1208